CIRCLES OF COMPASSION
A Collection of Humane Words and Work

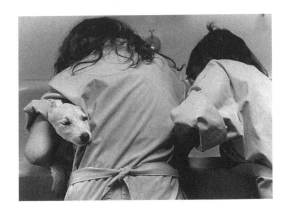

Edited by Elaine Sichel
Photographs by Sumner W. Fowler

VOICE & VISION
Publishing

Circles of Compassion: A Collection of Humane Words and Work

Edited by Elaine Sichel
Photographs by Sumner W. Fowler

Text Copyright © 1995 Elaine Sichel
Photographs Copyright © 1995 Sumner W. Fowler

Cover illustration by Adam Mathews
Cover and text design by Troy Scott Parker, Cimarron Design

ISBN 0-9643033-5-3
Library of Congress Catalog Card Number 94-61221

Published by:
VOICE & VISION Publishing
12005 Green Valley Rd.
Sebastopol, CA 95472

⊙ PRINTED ON ACID-FREE, RECYCLED PAPER

10 9 8 7 6 5 4 3 2 1

*The greatness of a nation and its moral progress
can be judged by the way its animals are treated.*

MOHANDAS GANDHI (1869-1948)

*I care not much for a man's religion whose dog
and cat are not the better for it.*

ABRAHAM LINCOLN (1809-1865)

To Terry's love,

Ray's memory,

my grandparents,

and every animal.

-Elaine Sichel

CONTENTS

ACKNOWLEDGMENTS

IF IT IS TO SUCCESSFULLY SPEAK for a diverse community, an anthology requires a great deal of enthusiasm, support, and most importantly, critiquing from members of that community. From the moment this book was conceived of, those needs have been generously met by a number of individuals and humane organizations. First and foremost, I must thank all of my former colleagues at the Marin Humane Society in Novato, California. During my tenure at this fine institution, and in the years that have followed, my passion for animals and their welfare has been continually sustained and enriched by the people who work there. It is a privilege to maintain an association with these true animal welfare professionals and an honor to be able to call them friends.

I wish to extend my profound gratitude to the hundreds of individuals who submitted material for this book when the call for entries was announced. While space limitations made it impossible to print a great deal of deserving work, I hope those whose work was not included will still feel represented. It is truly amazing—and deeply heartening—to know how many people are working so devotedly on behalf of companion animals. Reading their stories was without exception tremendously moving.

Special thanks must of course go to those whose work does appear in the book. The authors represented are a diverse group, representing many areas of the country and a variety of humane organizations. It is unfair to assign to them and their stories the burden of speaking on behalf of all humane shelters, their workers, and the animals they care for. Yet in a sense—at least for the purposes of this book—this is precisely the burden they must bear. By telling us the tales of animals they have known and worked with, the authors represented in this collection generously share with us a glimpse into a far larger world—that of the many millions of animals whose stories may never be heard. For this I am deeply appreciative.

My particular and considerable thanks go to those who read *Circles of Compassion: A Collection of Humane Words and Work* in manuscript form and provided suggestions and criticism. Rick Johnson, Pat Miller, Pam Williams, and Mickey Zeldes all provided helpful advice. Their combined years of experience in the animal welfare field and their insights certainly made this a better book. Special thanks also go to Mary Wright for reviewing the manuscript with her keen eyes and good judgement. While these individuals bear no direct responsibility for *Circles of Compassion* as it appears in its final form, I hope they do feel comfortable sharing some credit for it.

The written word can only go so far in depicting animals' beauty and the significance of our relationships with them. It is for this reason I am especially indebted to the photographer whose pictures appear in *Circles of Compassion*, Sumner W. Fowler. Many people take pictures of animals, but Sumner's photographs *give* us animals in all their splendor and joy. Through his portraits and candid shots we are able to feel the closest possible connection to animals—short of actually being with them. All the photographs featured are of sheltered or recently adopted animals. Sumner's work lends a dimension to this book that words on their own could not have achieved.

Finally, I'd like to thank some organizations that throughout the years have contributed to my ongoing understanding and appreciation of the human/animal bond. The Delta Society, The Humane Society of the United States, and The Latham Foundation have all enriched my work and provided enthusiastic support for this book. They, along with other important organizations and publications, are listed under Resources at the end of this book. I encourage everyone to support their important work.

– Elaine Sichel

INTRODUCTION

ELAINE SICHEL

ABOVE ALL ELSE, THIS BOOK IS a celebration, an affirmation, and most importantly, a declaration of hope. It is true that not all the stories that make up this anthology end on an upbeat note or provide the "happily-ever-after" conclusions we long for. But the accounts with less than idyllic endings, along with their more promising companion tales, achieve something larger—a greater good. The stories are like threads woven together to produce a vibrant and rich tapestry unmistakable in its theme: compassion. In animal shelters all across our country a cadré of thousands of devoted individuals work on behalf of millions of companion animals. The stories in this book tell only the tiniest fraction of these people's experiences and of the lives of the animals for whom they care. Forty-six stories can by no means represent a comprehensive picture of the world of humane action today. But what such a collection can do is, through a sampling of representative photographs, show and explain and share with all of us who care about animals the amazing and wide-ranging challenges and achievements, triumphs and tragedies, and deep sense of dedication and love of those who care for forsaken companion animals.

This is a collection of stories—all of them true accounts—by those working on behalf of forgotten or mistreated animals. One might quickly dismiss the value of such a volume, expecting it to be morose and banal, or peppered with resentment, bitterness and

anger. But the reader will find something quite different. These are
not stories of concession, or blame, or surrender, but of promise,
hope and commitment. No matter how great the odds seem or
how discouraging the path appears, those who work on behalf of
animals press on. Even in the face of sometimes seemingly unbearable heartache and discouragement, they keep to the tasks at
hand—caring for every animal they encounter and working to
make society more humane. How?

The answer to this question and the premise of this book are
one and the same. Compassion and the *humane ethic* are what keep
those in the humane field sustained. What is the humane ethic? It
is a means as well as an end, a way of thinking, a commitment,
and a goal. It is reflected in each piece in this book and called
upon by every author. Both the animals aided and the animals lost
are testimony to its importance. Compassion and the humane
ethic can be—and are—defined in a wide variety of ways among
those who work on behalf of companion animals. Yet their essential meanings are shared by all.

The origins of these values date back hundreds of years, and
have a rich and detailed history, accounts of which can be found
in books like E.S. Turner's *All Heaven in a Rage* and Gerald
Carson's *Men, Beasts and Gods* (see Resources). While the ethic
and philosophical arguments supporting it have existed for a long
time, it is in the animal sheltering movement that its fullest and
simplest expression is found. Animal shelters are the institutional
centers for the ethic of compassion. Their origin can be traced
back over one hundred and thirty years and across two continents.
Philosophers and humanitarians were already articulating and
promoting the theory that treating other species kindly was important, but it wasn't until the mid to late-1800's that activists like
Henry Bergh and George T. Angell (and many others) acted on
these sentiments and founded humane animal shelters such as the
American Society For The Prevention Of Cruelty To Animals

(ASPCA) in New York and the Massachusetts Society for the Prevention of Cruelty to Animals (MSPCA), respectively. (Few are aware that early efforts to prevent and legislate against child abuse were initiated by animal welfare reformers like these two men, and that today it is animal welfare activists who have established the link between childhood cruelty to animals and violent behavior towards fellow humans later in life). Similar efforts were undertaken in other major metropolitan areas across the United States. These pioneers, and those who followed, believed that without institutions to protect and promote the interests of animals and to offer the ones who were dispossessed a safe haven, we could never hope for a truly humane society. Thus the institutions—humane societies and societies for the prevention of cruelty to animals (SPCAs)—bore the same names as their goals.

Today's humane societies and SPCAs would scarcely be recognizable to the early activists. While animal shelters continue to carry on the traditional and essential functions of rescuing and housing animals in distress, they also provide a wide variety of other services. From the smallest all-volunteer shelter (some even lacking a physical shelter *structure*) to the largest metropolitan state-of-the-art facilities, humane organizations are busily engaged in a host of activities that support and assist the animals and animal owners in their communities. Adoption programs, pet lost and found services, municipal animal control functions, cruelty investigations, rescue and relief efforts during natural disasters, education programs for children of all ages, special low or no-cost programs to place companion animals with seniors, mobile outreach efforts, adult education courses, dog-training classes, low-cost spay/neuter, vaccination and veterinary clinics, legislative campaigns, and dog and cat licensing programs are just a few of the diverse services and activities today's humane shelters offer.

Unfortunately—despite the hard work of generations of caring individuals and great strides in the way companion animals are treated—the goals the founders of humane animal shelters espoused over a century ago have not been fully realized. Humane societies and SPCAs have not succeeded in putting themselves out of business. Certainly they have accomplished a great deal. Society now exhibits much more awareness, sensitivity and responsibility towards animals than the early activists could have ever predicted possible. But huge challenges remain. Animal shelters struggle to convince youth of the value of treating animals with kindness, pet overpopulation plagues every community in this country, and animals continue to be abandoned, neglected, mistreated and abused. And most sadly, as a consequence of all the other challenges and problems, *surplus* companion animals continue to be euthanized. The humane ethic sustains all those working on behalf of animals, but much of society has yet to learn the ethic's meaning or incorporate it into daily life. If such were the case, no one would ever again refer to a living animal as *surplus*.

But the bad news is only part of the picture, and while this book does not shy away from it, its primary purpose and ultimate goal is to celebrate what is possible. Even in the cases when an animal is not reached in time or saved or rehabilitated and death comes unjustly, there is one redeeming element: that someone who cared was there to aid them. The unnecessary death of even one companion animal is as one author notes, "a place we never should have come to." But finding ourselves there, it is at least comforting to know that a compassionate and humane hand and heart can be offered.

Those who work in animal shelters are without fail asked one particular question more than any other by usually well-intentioned inquirers: *If you love animals, how can you work here?* A more personalized version of the same question comes in the form of a declaration: *I love animals too much; I could never work here.* If one question or statement can sum up all of society's misunderstanding and confusion over the function of animal shelters and the motivations of those who work in them, these do. As each of the stories in this book attests to, those who work at humane shelters feel a love so strong for animals that they cannot imagine *not* working on their behalf. Yes, at times the heartache does nearly break them; but the miracle is that instead of giving up the people who tell their stories here, and the many others on whose behalf they speak, keep at it. They see the difference they are making reflected in amber or almond eyes, in joyous reunions, in rehabilitated bodies, in eased souls, or when they are defeated in their aims, a gentle passing. Precisely *because* they love animals so much and they know triumph is possible they keep on working on behalf of individual animals and the values of compassion and empathy.

One of the aims of this book is to make a link. A great many of us—and certainly those reading this book—are comfortable labeling ourselves "animal lovers." The label is often tossed around like some kind of credential or badge. For some it is almost a birthright with which they have been born. *"Oh yes, she a real animal lover…"* or, *"he's always been an animal lover."* This book is meant for anyone who has described themselves as such. If the connection can be made between those who profess an innate love for animals, and those who work in the places where forgotten animals receive shelter and care, humane societies can accomplish their goals. We are a nation of pet-lovers, and if we were to marshal our forces we could solve the problems of irresponsible pet ownership. This book is in part then a battle cry.

Pets present a curious paradox in our society. We own 600 million companion animals. Seventy-eight percent of households have at least one pet. We adore them. We spend billions of dollars annually on their care and entertainment. Fancying and breeding many species are popular pastimes. Growing up with a pet is considered by many a virtual requirement for normal family life. We celebrate our animals' birthdays, we give them endearing names,

we talk to them, carry pictures of them in our wallets, and when
the time comes, we memorialize their passing.

The irony, though, is that for every pampered and doted-upon
pet who lives out his or her life in a loving home, there are several
other animals who it seems are doomed from birth. They are part
of a litter that was unplanned. The offspring—baby bunnies,
hamsters, pups, kittens, chicks, *etc.*, are unvaccinated, untrained,
unaltered, uncared for, unincluded, *unwanted.* They never or for
only a short time know the comforts of a good home or kind word
or gentle hand. Sometimes the neglect is passive or benign; other
times, malevolent. In some instances the animal simply becomes
inconvenient, problematic, or "gets in the way." In other cases the
pet becomes a scapegoat, the target for displaced anger or rage.
Sometimes a person wishing to relinquish their pet displays a
glimmer of responsibility and brings the animal to a humane
shelter. More often though animals are simply left behind or
dropped off or locked up somewhere in the mistaken belief or
overt lie that they will survive on their own, or "someone else"
will take care of them. Only luck or fate bring such animals to a
shelter.

The stories in this book touch on many variations of the theme
of human betrayal. There are as many stories of betrayal as there
are animals passing through shelter doors (an estimated 10 to
25 million annually, depending on one's source of statistics). Some
come in as strays, but are never redeemed (where might a quiet
middle-aged hound or a matted fourteen-year-old Persian have
been living all these years?) The common betrayals. The standard
items on the inventory of "reasons for surrender." Cat left behind
in empty apartment. Dog left tied in yard when renters are
evicted. Kitten let loose because it was too playful. Dog dropped
on side of road—pregnant (again). Cat has litter—getting old and
too much trouble to care for, so they'll keep one of the kittens
(and turn in mom). The dog is too protective or not protective

enough. Or "I'd like to turn this cat in—can I maybe trade it for another one?" "I've got a donation for you—my dog just had puppies!"

These are the more commonly reported cases. Then there are more unique cases, the more overt, shameless manifestations of betrayal. An adult female Doberman with 100 BB pellets imbedded in her flank, used for target practice by a group of teenage boys. The kitten found dangling from a ceiling light cord, strung up by her two back legs, the light flickering on and off as she struggles. The dog, sexually abused by her deranged owner. The kitten, placed in an oven in a brown paper bag by a woman seeking vengeance against a former friend (the kitten sustains burns while the two argue, but miraculously survives). The abandoned dog, a litter recently delivered, wandering down the rain-soaked highway, a squirming pup clenched gingerly in her mouth.

In the last twenty years we have come to a far better understanding of ourselves in relation to other species. The environmental movement has sharpened our awareness and stimulated many of us to try to heal our relationship with Earth's other residents. We are more sensitive than ever to such issues as shrinking habitats, pollution, endangered species, overhunting, the illegal animal trade, and more. We have come to realize that our sense of empathy can and should embrace not just other humans, but all our fellow creatures. This book asks us to return to a decidedly simple premise though: unless we can improve the status of companion animals in our society—species we have domesticated and turned into pets—we have not, despite all our advances in consciousness, come very far. How we treat the animals closest to us tells us everything about ourselves and, as Gandhi said, "our greatness as a nation and…moral progress."

This book then is meant to serve as a testament, an inspiration, a signpost pointing us toward a better future for our companion animals. In stories like "Pippin" and "Penny's Shine" the book illustrates some stirring examples of victories for all animal lovers to celebrate, but in pieces such as "Caesar" and "For Gray Cat" it also tells the truth about animals who were not reached in time. In works such as "How Kato Was Rescued From the Superstition Mountains" and "Firestorm Diary" the book portrays the incredible compassion and accomplishments of those who work in animal shelters, but in stories like "Killing Them Softly" we are reminded there is still far too much to lament.

The purpose of this book and the sincere wish of all those whose stories appear in it is that everyone who reads *Circles of Compassion* come away with the desire—indeed the compulsion—to support local and national efforts to create a truly humane society. No gift greater than the granting of this wish could ever be bestowed upon our animals.

A resource section at the end of the book provides some information and suggestions on how readers can help contribute toward humane and companion animal welfare goals.

EDITOR'S NOTE

*A note on how the book is organized. It is divided into three
sections. The first section, "Remembering Legacies," tells the tales
of animals whose lives sadly ended, but whose legacies live on and
in whose memory many of the authors continue to work. Part II,
"The Making of Alliances," features accounts of successful and
entertaining reunions, adoptions and rehabilitations. The final
section, "Keeping Commitments," is a more eclectic assemblage of
essays, cases, and recollections by those working on the "frontlines"
of humane work.*

PART I

REMEMBERING
LEGACIES

The worst sin towards our fellow creatures is
not to hate them, but to be indifferent to them.
That is the essence of inhumanity.

GEORGE BERNARD SHAW (1856-1950)

Misty

ROSANN CLAY

ISTY CAME TO US as a surrender. The woman was
elderly, and although she had owned the cat since it
was a kitten, her family thought she should no
longer keep it. Their concern was that, because of
her age, their mother might trip on the animal that followed at
her heels so faithfully. Pressured by her loving children, the lady
signed Misty over to our shelter, breaking the heart of a cat who
had known no other human.

Who was Misty? She was the most beautiful smoke cream
Persian cat one could imagine. Her fur was long and silky and
since her owner had so enjoyed grooming and stroking the cat, it
was as soft as down. Misty's eyes were copper in color: clear and
knowing at their depth. She had been spayed and de-clawed at an
early age and had spent her life indoors, an "only cat" and well
aware of that special status. Arrogant, aloof and a lady all the way,
Misty suddenly found herself at an animal shelter, surrounded by
strange humans and even stranger sights and smells.

As was our policy for surrendered animals, Misty was placed in
a holding cage in our isolation area. She was terrified. The dogs,
housed in an adjacent kennel area, barked excitedly whenever
anyone came to see them. The forty or so cats on the premises
were of varying ages and sexes. There were usually several females
in season and great number of kittens, many unweaned, calling

and mewing throughout the day. Cleaning occurred every morning and visitors came every afternoon. Although Misty wasn't on the list of adoptable animals as of yet, she was in the midst of this constant activity. It proved too much for her; she stopped eating. Originally weighing in at eleven pounds, the staff had thought of her as a pampered, full-figured cat. But now that she was losing weight at an alarming rate, it was no longer a laughing matter. Misty was in full mourning for the owner she knew was not going to return. The special attention we gave her did not help. Tempting foods were offered, but Misty would eat only small amounts of dry food. She would not touch anything else. Additional feedings were scheduled and vitamin supplements were added to her food.

Still the cat lost weight. In desperation at the thought of losing such a beautiful animal who now weighed barely five pounds, the director of the shelter began an intensive socialization period with Misty. She would go into the isolation area with Misty three or four times a day, remove Misty from her cage and, while holding her gently in her lap, stroke and groom the pitiful little cat, speaking in only quiet, loving tones. The director lived close to the shelter, so she added an after-hours visit which often lasted in excess of half an hour. She also came to the shelter early in the morning before any of the staff had arrived, in order to have an additional bit of quiet time with Misty before another hectic day began. Misty began to respond.

Her recovery was nothing short of miraculous. Slowly at first and then with gusto, Misty began to eat. As she began to gain weight she also began to take a new interest in the many people that constantly came to check on her. She seemed to realize that once again she had achieved the status of "pampered pet." It was no secret that she had become a favorite of staff and volunteers alike.

Misty blossomed. Her weight hit twelve pounds and no one ever mentioned the word diet again. She would acknowledge her name whenever called with either a disdainful stare or a meow. She was allowed out of her kennel now for exercise but she chose to follow the staff around, rubbing against legs and begging to be groomed. When groomed, she would rattle the window glass with her purrs. The time had come for Misty to be placed on the adoption list. She was already spayed and her feline leukemia test result was negative, so she was admitted into the Open Room with the other cats. Adjusting to the change in surroundings took her no time. Misty chose her basket, curled up, and went right to sleep. There would be no more stainless steel quarters for this lady—it would instead be flannel and lamb's wool all the way! Misty was going to make it.

Misty was adopted about a month after moving into the Open Room. The woman simply fell in love with the beautiful cat with the long luxurious fur. After her adoption application had been approved, the woman came and picked Misty up to take her to her new home. We all felt sadness mixed with joy in a way that only a person working in an animal shelter and experiencing such partings can know. When Misty left us we had teary eyes but happy hearts.

Our joy was not to last. The woman tearfully returned Misty to us within two weeks. She had tried everything but she was apparently allergic to the long fur she so loved. She could not afford the allergy treatments and she could no longer stand the symptoms plaguing her constantly. Misty was returned to the Open Room.

This time Misty's grief was short-lived. About three days after her return, Misty began to eat and get on about her business. Staff noticed however that she was not using her litter box as fastidiously as she had previously. She was still good about using the litter to urinate, but she chose to defecate on the floor. Stressed more than we could have imagined, Misty was simply giving up in a different arena of her life. We realized immediately that this would greatly affect her adoptability but it was decided that in the right loving home, Misty would most certainly go back to using her litter box properly.

The second adoption took longer. A woman came to the shelter wanting an indoor-only cat and was sure Misty fit the bill. We, on the other hand, were not so inclined and tried to discourage the woman by pointing out that because of her long fur Misty would have to be groomed daily. The woman did not see this as a problem at all, and assured us that in fact it would be a pleasure to brush such a lovely animal. We were also very specific about Misty's poor litter box habits, but the woman agreed with us that, most likely, the cat just needed patience, understanding, and a loving home. She wanted Misty, despite all of our attempts to discourage her. Since the woman was married, we requested that her husband come in to meet the chosen animal, but the woman said her husband worked and would not be able to come. We were unable to get even his signature on the adoption form, but we did get his social security number, which gave us the needed confirmation that this was a legitimate adoption to which all parties had agreed. Being human, we made a mistake.

Several weeks after the woman had happily taken Misty to her new home, the woman's husband returned Misty. He stormed into the shelter, and oblivious to the other visitors present, literally threw a terrified Misty at the shelter director! Misty was uncontrollably hysterical. Her wide frightened eyes and pitiful yowls were heartbreaking. The man was also out of control, cursing and yelling, "Take your damn cat back. It doesn't do anything but s__t on the floor anyway." The staff lead him out of the shelter as quickly as possible while he continued to rant and rave about "that filthy cat."

Misty was a mess. She had feces caked around her tail, in addition to several badly matted areas in her fur that had to be cut out. Apparently, the cat had not been groomed since leaving the shelter. It took several staff members to contain Misty while we cleaned her. She fought as if for her very life. Afterward, she was placed back in the isolation area where her time with us had started. She remained withdrawn and frightened for weeks and we always believed that the violence we had witnessed that afternoon had more than once been directed at Misty. She had been abused, possibly beaten, because she would not use her litter box properly. It was decided that in the future anyone wishing to adopt Misty would have to spend time with her at the shelter so that we could see the interactions between the two parties. Furthermore, we would depend on our gut feelings and refuse anyone we didn't trust; Misty would be protected at all costs.

A long time passed. Then the university professor came to the shelter. He was not sure we could help him, but because he believed strongly in the purpose of animal shelters, he wanted to see if we could accommodate his rather specific requests for a new pet. He wanted an adult cat, a beautiful one if possible. Even more importantly though he wanted a cat that was not playful. The professor had a lovely home, with nice furnishings and an elaborate aquarium. He didn't want a cat that would run around the house wrecking havoc. And finally, the cat should match his color scheme of pale neutrals.

Normally we would have discouraged a person with such rigid notions from adopting an animal from the shelter. Typically they are looking for a pedigreed animal and nothing pleases them. In this case however, it was different.

It was love at first sight. "You beautiful little lady," he said, "what are you doing in there with all those other cats? You should have a penthouse suite all to yourself"—something Misty had been trying to convince us of for a long time. The man was given Misty's whole story, including the information about her continuing poor litter box habits, but he was not to be swayed. He came twice a week for the next three weeks to spend time with her. During each visit the staff observed from a distance. Both Misty and the professor seemed to deeply enjoy the visits. Finally, he could wait no longer. If we would agree to it, he wanted to adopt Misty. While the final forms were being completed, the gentleman crooned to the cat, "You sweet lady, Daddy's going to take you right home and give you a bath and a good brushing. You should see the pretty new basket waiting for you!" This was going to be a wonderful adoption for an animal whose life had been marked by such sadness. Tears were shed by all but the professor, who promised to keep us informed about Misty's progress and her new life. And he did.

At first all the reports were joyous. Misty had immediately set about claiming the Queen Anne sofa as her own; she spent not one minute in her new basket. The professor had shown her the aquarium, but Misty, always a lady, showed no interest. It came as a shock then one night when Misty suddenly leaped from the sofa and attacked a toy mouse the professor had given her some weeks earlier. For a minute he thought she might start playing. The move proved though to be only a temporary lapse in Misty's normally regal demeanor. She immediately jumped back up on the sofa, curled up next to the professor and fell back asleep—obviously worn out by the whole experience!

The man had addressed Misty's litter box problems by confining her to a tiled bathroom whenever he had to leave the house. She soiled the floor daily but it had been easy enough to clean up. After a while though, the man began to feel that such confine- ment amounted to little more than a bigger, lonelier Open Room. He decided to let her have the run of the house, so she would know she was a full member of the family, and hopefully resume her previous good litter box habits.

But it didn't work—indeed nothing worked. Six months had passed and Misty was still soiling the floor, but she now had a certain spot she preferred. In the living room/entrance hall of the professor's home was a large Oriental carpet. It came almost to the very edge of the front door, and it was in that area, by the door, that Misty chose to eliminate every day.

When the man entered the house, feces would be smeared across the carpet. He cleaned it every evening, but he was getting tired. He was also embarrassed whenever he considered bringing guests over from the University, concerned that he would have one of these messes to deal with as soon as he and his company entered the house. He was at the end of his rope when he called us. He didn't want to give Misty up but he did not want to make her a prisoner confined to the bathroom. He felt he had tried everything he could think of to entice Misty back to her box. Did we know of *anything* else he could try? Sadly, we did not and so the decision was made for him to return Misty to the shelter.

Misty looked wonderful! The professor had groomed her daily, so her fur was glossy and full. She had been eating very well and was heavier than we had ever seen her. She came out of her travel kennel and went right to the door of the Open Room. She peered through the screening as if to see which of her friends were still there. This time she did not appear to grieve over the loss of her home and, in fact, seemed almost happy to be back. We knew this was not a good sign. She was once again put in the isolation area to be observed, and then moved to the Open Room.

It was early November. Misty had spent spring and summer with the professor. Winter at the shelter had been difficult for Misty because of the short, dark days and the extreme and bitter cold outside which limited her activity. Likewise, we knew summertime at the shelter was also hard on Misty; there was no air-conditioning and although the Open Room had a window with a large attached cat run, there was rarely a breeze to cool the area. Misty would not go outside but instead lounged around in her basket, expending as little energy as possible. Despite all the care and comfort and love we could offer Misty, the shelter was no place for her to live out her life.

It was decided, in the end, to euthanize Misty. It was not an easily reached decision. There was much discussion and more than a few tears, but our purpose as an animal shelter is to relieve suffering, not prolong it. We had to consider what kind of life we were going to be giving Misty at that point. Furthermore, all her failed adoptions had made her chances for a successful placement virtually non-existent. She would be taking up valuable space in our crowded facility. We had accommodations for only forty cats and/or kittens and spring and summer saw our kennel capacity pushed to its limit. Misty's death might allow another cat a chance at life.

Misty was my favorite. Right or wrong, people in our profession form attachments when we know we shouldn't. I asked the director if, when the time came, I could have Misty's body. I just couldn't see her body being taken to the landfill. She was so beautiful and through no fault of her own her life had been filled with hardship. I wanted to give her a special resting place where I could check on her as often as I liked. The director granted permission and the date was set.

I lived in a rural area on six acres of land. In back of the house was a pond, a quiet place with a small knoll that looked down on the water. The area was alive with wildlife; birds, squirrels, rabbits, turtles. It was also home now to my old cat, euthanized the previous January. Misty would lie close to my Odin. I dug the grave.

On the appointed day, the director allowed me to come early and spend some special time with Misty until the staff was ready for her. As was our policy, we never had to assist in the euthanasia of our own favorites, but I carried her into the lab, stood by her and talked to her. She fought, as she did anytime she had to be restrained and that of course made the procedure more difficult for everyone. Because of all the movement, it took two attempts before the director was able to properly inject her. I was there to softly stroke her head as she rapidly slipped away from this world and into the next. I wrapped her in a flannel sheet and laid her in the box I had brought. The director asked if the prepared grave had room for two. I was puzzled, but said yes. She had decided it was also time to put down one of her own favorites and a buddy of Misty's. Misty and Hook had spent a lot of time together in the Open Room, so it was right that they spend eternity together. I wrapped Hook up and placed her in the box with Misty.

Misty was finally home. I buried them side by side and prayed. There would be no more cages, no more isolation or Open Rooms shared with other cats, no more miserable adoptions to people who could not understand that abused animals, like abused children, need extra love and patience, not scoldings or beatings. The knoll was quiet except for the singing of a few chickadees; Misty would have loved that but I knew where she was chickadees sang all year long.

Although she has been gone for over a year now, Misty's memory is always with me. Her photo hangs on the wall in my office and not a day goes by that I don't think of her. Her demise seemed so tragic and yet she was only one cat in a nation that euthanizes millions of animals yearly.

I went to a cat show recently and as I randomly wandered up and down the aisles, I suddenly found myself looking into copper eyes. There before me was a smoke cream Persian female, the very image of Misty and just for one brief moment, I hoped it was her. The cat made not a sound, just returned my stare with those same all-knowing eyes I'd seen in another time, another place. Her cage was well-decorated with ribbons, and in that moment, I realized just how fine a pedigree Misty must have possessed—but Misty was gone. I left the fancy show cat knowing that her fate would be so much better than Misty's. I was saddened that Misty had never had such a chance, but happy that this lady would. I turned back for just one more look and saw that she was now standing, facing me and ever so quietly I heard a single, soft meow. I smiled back at her and turned away.

A Dog Named Chase

CHERYL L. CUTSFORTH

I N MY MIND I ALWAYS call her Chase, for the merry one she led us on. I still think of her from time to time and probably will the rest of my life. The first time I saw her she was loping along the shoulder of Highway 53, north of Bloomer, Wisconsin.

A semi truck was hooting its horn shrilly, the driver certain she would run in front of his tires. She dodged, feinted, and darted across the two lanes of traffic just behind the truck. Her heart must have been pumping, adrenaline high. I know mine was. I stopped the car near her, opened the door and crooned to her, tempting her to come in out of the dangerous world. She cocked an ear at me but would come no closer. That night I put food out for her and drove home with a sinking feeling. No, it wasn't going to be easy to capture this one.

The second time I saw her she was sitting by the side of the road on the median, waiting and watching for someone or something. Maybe she scanned the horizon for the person who had abandoned her. Maybe she searched for any of the many volunteers who had put food out for her twice a day since we had first heard the report from the Humane Society of Barron County, nearly a week earlier, that a dog was living on the median, apparently unable to find her way out of the fences that lined the fields on each side of the highway. That night two of us brought out

beach towels and settled in to wait on the grass, quietly talking
and whispering sweet nothings to her. She ate the fragrant bacon-
flavored dog treats we laid out for her but stopped short of where
we could slip a leash over her head or coax her into the car. She
was interested in us, oh yes. But she wasn't ready for the risk of
actually letting us touch her, catch her, or as she may have
imagined in her mind, do unspeakable things to her.

After more than a week of attempts to win her over, we
requested help from the Eau Claire County Humane Association
since we did not own and could not afford a large-sized live trap.
Staff from the Eau Claire Animal Shelter were willing to help and
placed a carefully concealed, artfully baited live trap in the area
where we most often saw the dog. Twice each day volunteers
checked the trap. Bait ranged from gourmet canned dog food to
bacon-flavored treats to beef knuckle bones. In the end, and after
nearly two weeks of trying, it was plain old Milk Bones that won
her over and allowed her rescue. On a bright Wednesday afternoon
one of our board members stopped to check the trap, taking his
turn as we all grew more desperate to help her, more and more
certain that we were going to fail in our efforts to capture her. But,
there she was! Lured into the trap by the most ordinary of dog
treats. She growled softly that afternoon, hoping to frighten away
whoever came upon her in this helpless state inside the trap. The
volunteer spoke reassuringly to her and left to call for assistance.

Because the reactions of live-trapped animals are often unpredictable, the animals are usually released only after they have been
taken inside the shelter where they cannot escape again. Because
we did not have a vehicle large enough to carry this size live trap,
we again had to rely on Eau Claire County Animal Shelter staff.
They arrived promptly with their shelter van and took Chase in.

The next time I saw her she was lying on the floor of her
kennel, her tail slowly thumping. She was in reasonably good condition after all those weeks on her own, thanks in part I know to

the many volunteers who delivered food to the median regularly. She had been covered with ticks when she came in; marks where they had been were still visible. We chatted a bit, she and I, about how hard life is out on your own. I don't think she really liked it out there very much.

As it happened, that was the last time I saw Chase. She had to be euthanized. We had not, after all, reached her in time. Her fear, whatever things had happened to her before we met her, had defeated her. She was a biter. Shelter staff found her unpredictable. Volunteers soon learned not take her out of her kennel alone. Perhaps, with time and endless patience and an experienced hand to train her she might have learned not to strike out at people. But homes like that are hard to find and the shelter's responsibility to the public made it impossible to place her. The risk of her biting someone, perhaps seriously, was just too great. With far fewer homes than there are pets waiting to be adopted, those who do find homes are usually the prettiest, the ones without handicaps or battle scars, the sweetest, the ones without psychological wounds from past ill treatment or neglect, the youngest, the ones without much experience in the world. Chase was young, no more than eighteen months, and she was pretty, a petite yellow lab mix. But her psychological scars were deep and damaging. They made her unsuited for the average home, so she paid the price of her life for the cruelty of the person who dropped her off on that highway one day in May.

Yes, I will think of Chase sometimes for all the rest of my days.

THIS ACCOUNT IS DEDICATED to the volunteers who fed Chase and checked her live trap faithfully twice a day for many weeks. Their work was not in vain. Because of them, Chase did not die slowly of rabies or distemper, or lie in the woods, injured by a car, her life seeping painfully away. She did not bring more puppies into a world already too full of unwanted ones. She did not grow colder or stiffer as autumn passed and winter came, freezing to death at the last, or die from a bullet, after learning to chase cattle or deer in her boredom living along the highway. Although this story did not have a happy ending, it is one told by every humane society across the country. Humane volunteers gave Chase what may have been the only true compassion she was to know in her young life. If animals are reborn, may Chase return as the cherished housepet she deserved to be.

Caesar

THERESE C. MACKINNON

AESAR, A "STRAY" CAT, was euthanized today. I use the word stray in the loosest of terms, because, contrary to popular belief, cats very seldom stray from home. They're much too provincial for that sort of thing. More likely, that scraggly looking cat you see wandering through your yard has been abandoned, or it is the offspring of such a cat. Its family may have moved away, having decided that it was inconvenient to pack the cat along and that it would surely "find" another home. Or the cat may have been intentionally discarded when it reached maturity and began marking its territory and fighting, or when it became pregnant. Of course, these problems could easily have been solved with a simple spay or neuter operation.

Seldom does a cat choose to leave its home territory, so when a nameless, yellow, unaltered male cat was brought in to the animal shelter one morning in a wire trap it was no surprise to hear the bearer say that his neighbors had moved away, leaving kitty behind.

The man set the trap down by the counter. Huddled tensely in the steel mesh box, eyes wide with terror, the little animal didn't look like much, just another scared vagabond. I took down what sketchy information the neighbor could offer. The cat was about four-years-old—not so old—not, that is, until placed in a shelter, surrounded by cuddly, highly adoptable kittens. He had been on his own for several weeks and had been fighting with every cat in the neighborhood. He had the distinct musk odor of an unaltered male feline. Age, behavior and sex, I thought: three strikes, you're out. He was the classically unadoptable cat.

As I brought him into the holding room and set him up in a clean cage, I wondered what his personality would reveal once he settled in with us. Well, Caesar, as he was soon to be dubbed, was trouble from the very start, and it was not long before I was hopelessly in love.

He was a yellow tabby—yellow, not like buttercups or tangerines, but subtle, like cornmeal. He was compact and solid, all muscle, all tomcat, yet his fur was as soft as cotton balls and thicker than lamb's wool. His coat was short and silky along his flanks and he had a long ruff around his neck that made him look like a handsome young lion. The fur on his belly was thick and downy and, oh, his tail! It was magnificent, dense and bushy so that pieces of litter and food were always getting caught up in it. I was constantly combing it out with my fingers. Diagonally across his nose and cheeks was painted a single white stripe, rather like the make-up of an Indian brave.

Caesar had clear, round eyes, yellow, the color of his fur. They weren't the kind of eyes that you might say, "could see right through you." Not at all. He wasn't a wise sort. But he was dashing and devil-may-care, and when I looked in his eyes and he gazed back at me, I knew that he trusted me and considered me his friend.

As I said, Caesar was trouble from the start. We all knew it the day he began picking the latch on his cage door and taking nightly excursions through the corridors of the shelter. We would come in mornings to find him staring down at us happily from some shelf or curled up on a pile of blankets in a storage cabinet. Murphy-Cat, our wimpy shelter mascot, never turned up with any wounds after these evenings of freedom, so I suppose they either never met or Caesar preferred exploring to ravaging. I like to think the latter. When we finally got wise and put a lock on his cage, Caesar began picking the latch on the door next to him. My little freedom fighter: if he couldn't be footloose, he was going to see to it that someone else was.

Although Caesar was a mature adult cat, he still had the heart of a kitten. That which remained still, was sniffed and passed by. But that which moved, or growled, or just looked inviting, was fair game for a pounce. It made perfect cat sense. One day, Carole, my co-worker, was moving a cat with an exceptionally fluffy and inviting tail. She passed too close to Caesar's cage, and he, always the opportunist, grabbed it—and tenaciously refused to let go. The more the poor gray Persian wailed, the more worth keeping hold of her tail. Caesar was finally persuaded, forcibly, to give it up. But the second time he grabbed someone, a sweet little black Angora, I knew his days were numbered. However, being not so wise, and not inclined to change for anyone, Caesar remained full of the mischief that was to be his undoing.

One day a young couple came in, hoping to adopt not one, but two adult cats! They had recently lost their cat to feline leukemia, a deadly disease. After looking at all of the available candidates, they chose Wiggins, a neutered, buff-colored Angora, and Caesar. This was the one chance for adoption that had come Caesar's way in the two months and a day that he had been with us. Knowing his impetuous nature, we feared there might be bloodshed, but wanting dearly for him to find a home, we decided to give it a try. We brought both cats and the couple into a visiting room to see how they would all get along. As we placed the cats on the floor in opposite corners, their eyes met. I held my breath and waited, tensed to intervene, should there be trouble. The cats ran straight at each other, sniffed a greeting and then, began to explore the room! I breathed a heavy sigh of relief—and then it happened.

Caesar, with his flare for the unexpected, spied a mama cat nursing her three kittens in a nearby upper cage, and leaped. He leaped six feet in the air and landed vertically on the bars of the cage. The terrified mother cat, determined to defend her brood to the end, hissed and lashed with all her might, but Caesar held fast. As far as he was concerned, this was fun! The horrified couple looked on as we pried him from the bars and carried him back to his cage. They later adopted Wiggins and Whitey, both neutered males, highly adoptable and very lucky animals indeed.

I'd like to say that someone came in that very day, saw something in Caesar and realized that he was just the companion they were looking for. Or maybe I could say that the owner finally came in to claim him, their beloved long-lost pet. I'd love to say that I or one of the other shelter staff members was able to rescue him at the last moment and take him home to be our very own. But the reality is that there are just too many animals and not enough homes for them all. Pet breeding is out of control. It's not the fault of Caesar or any of the animals that come in to the hundreds of shelters across the country. It's something that only we, the pet owners, can do anything about. We must take the responsibility for curbing the thousands of unwanted domestic animal births that occur every day in our own little corners of the world. And we must make a lifelong commitment to the pets we chose to keep.

Caesar's fate was sealed that day, through no fault of his own. The next day he was placed on the list for euthanasia. Euthanasia is a Greek word in origin. Literally it means "good death" and is described as the act of killing painlessly for reasons of mercy. I wonder who the Greeks did it to, and how they did it and was it really painless or did they just prefer to hope or wish it was, as we do at the animal shelter.

We killed several animals that day, two months and two days after Caesar had arrived. There were two dogs, seven cats, three kittens and a rabbit. Two of the animals were old and sickly; the kittens were too young to survive in a shelter environment. The rest of the animals, one puppy, six cats, including Caesar, and the rabbit were killed simply and senselessly because no one wanted them. Too many animals, not enough homes.

That afternoon, I held Caesar in the corridor and waited for the veterinarian to finish with the rabbit. He lay in my arms, squinting up at me peacefully, purring as I scratched his neck and clucked at him. I thought, maybe it will be okay, maybe he won't struggle and it will be quick. But deep inside I knew that Caesar would not give up his life so easily and I really expected nothing less of him.

It took four hands to restrain him on the table, to stop his thrashing, to silence his objections as the veterinarian pumped what seemed like a horse's dose of sodium pentobarbitol into his veins. He did not die a good death, because death is never good outside of the natural order of things. Caesar was a victim of someone's thoughtlessness or perhaps just the simple ignorance of a society that thinks of other living creatures as objects, to be used for a while and then discarded. But if we would truly look into the eyes of another living being, our souls would be changed. We would realize their incredible worth. Like all living creatures, Caesar was unique, he was one-of-a-kind, I loved him, and he will never be again.

The Sentinel

RONNETTE FISH

A flicker by the roadside, a rustle in the grass,
a greyness quickly darting 'cross the rise.
A whisper softly moving, a light stir of the wind,
The lonely sound of faint and troubled cries.

A whimper from the gully, a shadow on the bridge,
A turn—and what was there has ceased to be.
A spot beneath the stone arch, dry weeds worn down from rest,
The tracings of a life we cannot see.

>And the Sentinel is watching
>From the shadow
>Of the old bridge
>In the darkness, always waiting
>By the bridge.

A tale of life abandoned, sweet love left on the road,
A trusting heart cast cold upon the wind.
In innocence she waited, watching by the thicket
For their return to take her home again.

A car's approach would bring her swiftly from the trestle.
Her eager eyes alert upon the lane.
The stranger's glance in passing would start to see the figure
Of a mongrel dog standing in the rain.

And the Sentinel is watching
From the shadow
Of the cold bridge
In the darkness, always waiting
By the bridge.

It's long since she was last seen watching by the roses'
Thick wild blooms along the prairie way.
Her loyal form is missing, the ragged ghost at rest;
An unloved friend has sadly passed away.

Yet, the path has not grown over where she would patrol,
The spot beneath the arch still sparse and worn.
A spirit seems to wander just beyond the roadway,
Vigilant at the bridge from morn to morn.

And the Sentinel is watching
From the shadow
Of the stone bridge
In the darkness, always waiting
By the bridge.

A FEW YEARS AGO a short distance outside of a small town not far from Sioux Falls, South Dakota, a dog was abandoned. The Sioux Falls Humane Society received many calls on this dog on the highway, always in the same spot by a bridge. However, the dog was extremely shy, and if approached or pursued, she was quickly gone. She would always return to the same spot at the bridge though. This continued throughout the summer, until one day she vanished. She was never again seen. Her body was never spotted; she had simply disappeared. "The Sentinel" is her story, and it is one repeated all too frequently across our nation's highways.

Kitten Season Again

PAT MILLER

"Please tell me you won't kill them,"
    the kitten's owner cried.
"I couldn't bear to tell the kids
    that Fluffy's babies died!"

"Just look how wonderful they are,
    all snuggled in their box…
One calico, one tiger-stripe,
    one gray with four white socks."

"We promised when we got the cat
    that we would get her spayed,
but we were just too busy;
    the appointment got delayed."

"Before we even knew it
    little Fluff was getting fat…
Pregnant at just six months old,
    can you imagine that?"

"And then, of course, we realized
    the kitten's lives were worth
the chance to let our kids enjoy
    the miracle of birth."

"We tried real hard to find them homes
      but it was pretty tough.
No one seemed to want to take
      these precious balls of fluff."

She gave each kitten one last kiss
      and left them with a sigh.
She missed the tear that trickled
      from the corner of my eye.

I knew, like thousands come before,
      who had no better fared,
these kittens soon would die
      within the arms of those who cared.

But as the lady reached the door
      she turned and cleared her throat,
and against all crazy odds
      my heart stood still with hope.

Perhaps she'd reconsidered,
      perhaps she'd changed her mind.
Perhaps she knew she had a chance
      to prove she could be kind.

But fleeting hopes were quickly dashed;
      reprieve was not to be,
for when she opened up her mouth
      the lady said to me,

"Did I forget to tell you
      that Fluffy's in the car?
We've decided we don't want
      her either anymore."

Sage – "Gentle, Leads Well, Loads OK"

RONNETTE FISH

THE SUM OF TWENTY YEARS and that's all we knew about her. She was terribly emaciated, nothing but bones, the remains of last winter's coat still not completely shed. Her mouth was full of sores; the sharp points of her teeth had not been filed for a long time. Had her whole life been one of neglect and hunger, or had she been a well-cared for horse and just sold into the wrong hands?

At the Humane Society we preach the importance of spaying and neutering dogs and cats because of overpopulation. Not enough homes for all the litters of puppies and kittens born. However, the problem of too many horses being bred is just as serious. The result is horses trucked to slaughterhouses by the hundreds and thousands. These are not just old, broken down horses. They are registered Arabians, Quarter Horses, Saddlebreds, and others; young, well-trained horses that are healthy and have been well-cared for. They go to slaughter houses because the "killers" can outbid those who just want a riding horse. Horse meat for human consumption sells well in Europe and Japan, and it is used in canned pet food in the United States.

Perhaps Sage was a 4-H horse, well cared for by a young girl or boy going through a first horsemanship class. Had the child progressed on to another horse, and no longer needed Sage? Had that same child patted her on the neck, said, "good girl, Sage" and never thought about her again after the horse trailer had pulled away with her? As she aged and the points on her teeth created sores so painful it hurt to eat, had her pain been simply ignored? Was she penned in a dry lot with a minimum of care, or had she been left in a pasture and forgotten?

At the end of her life Sage found herself in the arena of the local sale barn. As sick, tired and old as she was, she would still run through the arena. Sale barn workers are not known for their kindness towards the animals in their care. They prod, whip and beat the animals to move faster. One can only hope that at some point in their lives they will know the treatment they have inflicted upon these creatures of God.

A woman sitting in the arena was at once horrified at the condition of the horse and felt great compassion for her. Not even the killers bid on her, so the woman paid $27.50 for the bones running by, knowing full-well that the animal had no monetary value. The woman tried to get the name of the former owner from the sale barn, but she was told they did not have it. Indeed! The barn would sell a horse for someone and not get their name?

She brought the horse home. Her husband took one look at the horse demanded she get rid of it. The couple raised horses, and he could not afford to have people see a horse in such condition on his property. He was afraid someone would report *him* to the Humane Society. The woman called us and asked if we would take her. Of course we said yes.

The next day the woman pulled up with a horse that was starving to death because she could not eat. It was early afternoon. After unloading Sage and making her comfortable, we immediately called the veterinarian. He said he would try to make it out that evening, but the state veterinarians were having their annual meeting in Sioux Falls and so he wasn't sure he'd make it. The horse had obviously been in this condition for some time. Would another day make a difference? As it turned out, yes. That evening

Sage went down and we couldn't get her up again. The next afternoon the veterinarian did come, and he recommended what we
expected: immediate euthanasia. Months of neglect had taken its
toll; euthanasia would be best for her. So with the prick of a
needle, and the last movement of a leg, Sage finally found relief
from her pain.

King's Ransom

KIMBERLEE CURTIS

"**B**ASE ONE TO UNIT EIGHT," my radio cackled, "See the man at ABC Gravel Pits about a pack of feral dogs."

"Damn," I muttered to myself as I swung the old Ford around the block. I had just turned in my city police radio and had been ready to call it a day. ABC Pits was out near the marshes where legendary dog packs had run for years, and my senior officer's words about previous "pack" calls rang in my ears.

"These packs have run as long as I can remember. They're a constant problem, you can't get near 'em, they know the trucks, and trapping just doesn't work with 'em."

The sun was beginning its descent into glorious cascades of red and orange as I crossed over the river and passed into the notorious "southside." It wasn't an area I wanted to spend any amount of time in, especially without my police radio. School kids and drug dealers hung out on the same corners. My truck brought hostile glances and catcalls.

As the truck bounced across a set of railroad tracks, I saw a puff of gray dust lingering in the air. Acres of stone mounds signaled I was in the right place.

A grizzled old man hobbled out of a ramshackle tin building. "Ovah heh, ovah heh!" His eyes had a rheumy film of age, compounded by a distinct cast in two directions.

"Howdy, ma'am. I sure does 'preciate your comin' out heh today. Dese heh dawgs, dey come by and did triet ta git me. Dey come 'roun here lots, but dey never came afta me befoe. I don wanna git bit. Dey come too close today." He pointed to an overgrown lot filled with junk of all sorts.

I asked my standard routine of questions: Where exactly? How many dogs? What time? With each response I felt myself growing more guilty for my initial reaction to the situation. The hunchback old man was a gentle, kind soul. He was truly afraid of the dogs.

While I didn't really expect to find anything noteworthy, I explained I'd search the area and would return with a trap the next day. I knew I'd be mocked at the shelter, but I figured I didn't have anything to lose by trying to help.

I climbed back in the truck and followed a narrow dirt track between rusted carcasses of steamshovels and bulldozers. I stopped near a pile of exhausted tires, and saw a path beaten down in the weeds.

It ran through a small break in the chain link fence. I saw five mongrels of varying sizes darting across the distant marsh, stopping only to glance over their shoulders at me. I followed footprints around piles of scrap metal, and peered under a corroded sheet.

Two yellow eyes met mine. He laid there silently, gaze unwavering. His head was massive, and from the looks of his crossbreeding, there was Doberman running strong in his genes.

With a sinking stomach, I trotted back to my truck and reached behind the seat for my control stick. How would I ever capture this feral dog? While I never used my size—115 pounds—as an excuse for anything, there were physical limitations to my strength, and I knew the fury of a snared and cornered dog.

Expecting the worst, I gingerly inserted the stick down along the length of the metal sheet. I fully anticipated bared teeth and a full charge from the hulking beast.

Instead, he laid there, never moving a muscle until the noose of the control stick slipped over his head. I snapped the rope snug and braced for a charge. I ended up having to give a tug.

"Hey, buddy, c'mon and see me," I called to him softly.

He inched forward towards me and stood erect as he cleared the metal "roof" of his shelter. At least three-feet-tall at the shoulder, his head reached my beltline.

His sunbaked coat had once been a chocolate red; now it was dried and caked with mud. Grape-sized ticks covered his body, and his ribs had the gaunt look of life on the run.

As we stood facing one another, metal control pole between us, I felt one of the deepest communications with an animal that I had ever experienced. I swear to this day: that dog's eyes begged me to take him. From that moment, my fear vanished. This dog sought only peace.

I loaded him onto the truck and stroked him until the sun passed the horizon. Despite the fate that awaited him, I knew Buddy was ready to go home. The heartworms that plagued his body had done irreparable damage, and he was too worn to continue.

Three days later, Buddy's peace came. They said he stood proudly and quietly, and died with the dignity that befitted a king. To me, he was.

To Piper Sue

PAT MILLER

A pixie face staring solemnly through
the bars in the cage in the back
caught my attention one summer day
and stopped me dead in my tracks.

"What's her story?" I asked the staff
and I listened to their reply:
"They rescued her from a sewer pipe.
If they hadn't she would have died."

"She's awfully scrawny," I commented.
"Dirty and full of fleas…
I wouldn't get your hopes up too high,
we can't save many like these."

But something in the kitten's eyes
touched my heart and stayed in my head.
It was hard to envision her tiger-striped coat
lying there, cold and dead.

But I hadn't counted on shelter staff
or the wonders their love could do.
For they took the little one under their wing,
the kitten they named Piper Sue.

And when I checked back on the following day
a miracle had occurred.
They'd coaxed her to eat, and given her baths.
Now I watched while she happily purred.

So now we had to wait for a week,
the time that we give to strays.
And as we watched her valiant fight
we anxiously counted the days.

At the end of the week the prognosis was poor;
her condition hadn't improved
And yet while the rest of us started to grieve,
and officer's heart had been moved.

Although death was the obvious option
one person wouldn't say die.
So with Joy in our hearts Piper Sue headed home,
to give life another try.

The kennel staff hugged her and kissed her good-bye
and gave her a last farewell glance,
and then turned and went back to the kennels to find
another that needed a chance.

You ask me how I can love them,
and work here day after day.
I ask you how you can say you care
when you turn and walk away.

There are days of sadness, grief and despair,
anger and rage, it's true.
But I work here for the days we can help
the ones like Piper Sue.

DESPITE ONGOING VETERINARY CARE and the love and care of a real home with Marin Humane Society Officer Joy Lloyd, Piper Sue could not overcome her poor start in life, and died of medical complications a week after leaving the shelter.

Beansi's Tale

JOAN V. CHADWICK

SNOW WAS FALLING LIGHTLY when Beansi came out from under the shed where he had spent the night. It was deep, and he had to lift his paws high to clear the snow which brushed against his belly. When he reached the porch steps and saw the empty bowl at the top, he knew that the man had still not been to feed him. He meowed outside the door, but no one came. The woman had been gone a long time now, and whenever the man opened the door, Beansi would run quickly through the house to see if she had come back, and rush out again before he closed it. Beansi hated being indoors.

He sprang to the top of the fence which separated his yard from the neighbor's and looked around. The neighbor's cat, who hated Beansi, was nowhere in sight, so he jumped down, landing gently in the snow, and trotted up to the back door. He tested it with his nose to see if it would open, but it was shut tight. Sometimes the door would open, and when it did Beansi would run to the dish in the basement and grab a few bites before being discovered and chased out. The neighbor's cat usually left food in her dish, and often her humans cooked special food for her—something Beansi never got where he lived.

Today, all was quiet at the neighbor's, although the cat could now be seen sitting in the window eyeing Beansi suspiciously. The man who lived in this house would often be outside shoveling snow or working on his car, but he wasn't around today. He would talk to Beansi and scratch his ears.

Beansi was a large orange tom, with dark oval markings. His coat was long and matted. When the woman had first seen him, she said that he looked like he was covered in baked beans, and since he was also "full of beans," the name Beansi stuck. Most of the neighbors liked him because of his independent character, but he terrorized their cats, who were mostly pampered pets who never ventured far past their doorsteps. Beansi was fearless and a story had gone around the neighborhood that one day, confronted by large Doberman, Beansi had bristled up, hissing, tail erect and fluffed out, and stood his ground against the fearsome looking dog. Word had it that the dog had backed up and run in the opposite direction! The woman laughed when she heard this story, and told Beansi what a big strong boy he was. Beansi never had to fight with any of the neighborhood cats; his presence alone intimidated them enough so that they would abandon their special tidbits to him.

After waiting outside the neighbor's door long enough to know no one was home, Beansi set off on his usual rounds. It was one of those typical dark winter weekend mornings when people stayed in their houses most, if not all, of the day. A few cats were out in their yards or perched on doorsteps; but there was no food to be seen anywhere.

Across the street from where Beansi lived was a tropical plant conservatory. Beansi often visited the parking lot here to sit on the hoods of parked cars, enjoying the warmth generated by their recently turned-off engines. Sometimes visitors returning to their cars would pet him or murmur about what a handsome cat he was. He enjoyed the attention. Beansi crossed the street, strolled over to the nearest car, and hopped up on the hood. He positioned himself carefully on the bare spot where the engine had melted the snow. It was warm, and the cat lay on his belly, front paws tucked under his chest, and dozed.

When he heard approaching voices, Beansi raised his head, twitched an ear and squinting ever so slightly, looked around. When he saw two people coming towards him, he sat up and began to purr. Most people fussed over the large friendly cat they found sitting on their car, and this couple was no exception. As they stroked and petted him, Beansi stood up, arched his back, and rubbed against their bodies. He was hungry and thought they might possibly give him some food. He was surprised then when the woman picked him up and, talking to him softly, put him in the back seat of the car! Before Beansi knew it, the car was pulling away from the parking lot.

Beansi had been in a car only a few times, usually to be taken to a place where he would be poked and prodded by strangers and then brought back home. He had not enjoyed these outings, especially after the woman started putting him in a carrying box. That was after his first visit when he heard the dogs barking and jumped out of the woman's arms before they had gone inside. He had hidden under the steps of the strange place for quite some time before being coaxed out with a treat. Since then he had lost his fear of dogs, and he was no longer startled by their barking. Beansi thought that perhaps these people were taking him to that same place now, or perhaps they were just going to get food. The two talked in the front seat, and every once in a while the woman reached back to stroke Beansi and scratch his ears.

When the car stopped, the woman got out but the man stayed behind the wheel with the motor running. When the woman returned there was another woman with her, carrying a large plastic crate. She opened the back door, and pushing the crate ahead of her, spoke encouragingly to Beansi. He smelled a tantalizing aroma. They had brought food after all! He followed his nose to a dish filled with the kind of soft flavorful food the neighbors' cats were all fed. Before Beansi had a chance to taste the delicate morsels, the crate door was shut and the woman was carrying him into the building. The sound of barking dogs filled his ears, followed by the meows of more cats than Beansi could count. The door of the crate was then opened and Beansi found himself in a cage with a blanket, litter-box and dishes of food and water. He was exhausted. He lay on the blanket, curled into a ball and quickly fell asleep.

Later when he woke he made short work of the cat food. People came in and out of the room. His cage was cleaned, more food and clean water were placed in his bowls, and his litter box was changed. Beansi had never had much use for litter boxes. As an outdoor cat he had access to all the neighborhood flower beds and vegetable gardens he needed. But being a typically fastidious feline, and having no other choice, he now used this one when the need arose. The people, mostly female, were friendly, and some allowed him the run of the cat room while they cleaned his cage. There were a variety of cats in the other cages: frightened kittens who backed away when they saw the large tomcat; a huge black-and-white creature with enormous yellow eyes; a huffy Siamese; and a ragged old gray tom with frostbitten ears and a twitching tail Beansi carefully avoided. He remembered a fight the previous winter with a similar looking cat. The altercation had been followed by one of the visits in the car to the strange place, and he had felt odd for some time afterward. Newcomers came into the room, while others were taken away and did not return. Beansi lay in his cage, waiting for the woman to come and take him back to his familiar haunts.

After parking his car behind his sister's garage, Ed MacDonald plowed his way through the snow to the back steps. After he fed the cat, he'd better shovel the sidewalk. He'd meant to come yesterday, but his car wouldn't start, and by the time he'd got it going he was too tired. What the heck anyway, he thought. He wasn't worried about the cat—he was always scrounging for food in the neighborhood anyway. One day wouldn't kill him. Besides, Ed hadn't seen Beansi for a few days. He wasn't worried though. The food he put out was always gone. He'd be glad when June came back from her vacation in Mexico. He was getting sick of driving over every day. He couldn't understand what June saw in the cat anyway. He never stayed around, and he didn't like being indoors. Ed had tried to shut the door on him, but he always managed to get out. Ed didn't have a pet himself—too much trouble—but he promised June he'd look after Beansi while she was away. She'd looked forward to this trip for a long time. He opened the porch door, grabbed the dry cat food, and filled the empty dish after knocking the snow out of it. Ed shoveled the sidewalk, put the shovel back in the garage, and got in his car. If he hurried, he might just be able to catch the hockey game on TV.

Liz Blackburn was returning from work when she saw Ed's car pulling away from behind her neighbor's garage. Why June had trusted her lazy brother to look after Beansi was beyond her. She would have done it herself, but she'd been out of town on business, and her husband Brian had been gone almost a month now doing a film on location. She'd gotten in late Saturday night and stayed in bed late into the morning Sunday. By the time she gone outside to clear the snow she'd noticed that Beansi's dish on June's top step was empty. Beansi was nowhere to be seen, but then he could have been anywhere. Liz often had to chase him out of her own basement, where he would run in if the door was open or even slightly ajar and eat her own cat Mickey's leftover food. Beansi was well-known to most of the neighbors, but Liz didn't encourage him to come around because Mickey always cowered under the bed for hours after an encounter with the big tom. Come to think of it, Liz thought, she hadn't seen Beansi at all since she'd gotten back, and it was now Monday night. He'd probably turn up now that Ed had left his food.

The next morning Liz was late as usual and hurrying out to her car, when she noticed a magpie eating out of Beansi's dish. She decided it was time to look into the cat's whereabouts. Beansi was too smart to have gotten himself run over, and anyway someone on the street would have noticed something. She'd phone Ed when she got a chance, and go from there. Liz was beginning to worry about June's cat.

Things were slow at the office in the afternoon, so Liz decided to head home early. She called Ed, who said he hadn't seen the cat for over a week, but the food was always gone. He'd only missed one day when his car broke down. Liz hung up, put on her coat and headed out the door.

When Liz caught up with her, Mrs. Armstrong was just coming back from her daily walk. Liz asked her if she'd seen Beansi lately, knowing that the Armstrong residence was one of Beansi's regular ports-of-call. The elderly woman said she hadn't seen him in a while. The last time she remembered seeing him was a week ago Saturday. He was over in the greenhouse parking lot sitting on the hood of a car. She remembered seeing a couple petting him, and he seemed to be enjoying it, but then her phone had rung and by the time she hung up she'd forgotten about the cat. June's brother was looking after him, wasn't he?

As Liz walked home she thought about what Mrs. Armstrong had said. Maybe the couple had taken Beansi, although that seemed unlikely. He was friendly, but he was pretty rough looking. Not the kind of cat someone would just take home. There could be another explanation though. Back in her kitchen, Liz got out the phone book and looked up the number for the local animal shelter. The receptionist who answered the phone said the day staff had just left and she'd just come in, but there had been a cat there yesterday that matched Beansi's description. He'd been there over a week and they were surprised no one had claimed him, because he was such a friendly guy. A couple had brought him in; they'd found him wandering around a plant conservatory parking lot. He was bedraggled and hungry, and they thought someone had dumped him there, or maybe he'd jumped out of a car. He was quite a hit with the shelter staff, but they were short of room and couldn't keep him much longer. If Liz could come in right away to see if it was Beansi they'd really appreciate it.

When Liz arrived at the shelter it was dark and beginning to snow. The receptionist said the cat she thought might be Beansi was a real character. He'd prowl the cat room, even jumping into empty cages and eating leftover cat food while the attendants cleaned his cage. That sounds like Beansi, Liz thought, relieved that the mystery of Beansi's whereabouts appeared to be solved.

The receptionist headed to the back of the shelter to get the cat Liz thought was Beansi. After what seemed like a very long time she returned, empty-handed and looking puzzled. She pulled a thick file from her desk and pored over it carefully. Finally she looked up at Liz. Liz could see the sadness in the woman's eyes. She was terribly sorry, but the cat had been euthanized that morning. He had been there over a week—well over the normal (and legally required) amount of time the shelter held stray cats—and there were so many cats coming in there hadn't been room to keep him any longer. It was a shame. He was such a wonderful cat. This happened all too often. If only people looked after their cats better.

As Liz drove home through the snow, wiping the tears from her eyes, she thought about the events that had led to Beansi's end. June hadn't worried about him being left outside because he hated being indoors anyway, and the neighbors were all used to him roaming around anyway. It wasn't unusual for him not to be seen in his yard for a couple of days. The magpies had eaten Beansi's food on the days Ed noticed it was gone, and the snow had covered their tracks. Ed wasn't the worrying type anyway, and it hadn't helped that she and Brian had both been away. They were the ones most likely to notice Beansi's absence. Mickey was left alone too much these days too, and Liz promised herself she'd spend more time with her from now on. June was going to be upset, and the neighborhood would never be the same.

In My Dreams

GINA RICHEY

Don't close the door
*   don't push me away*
Why are you leaving?
*   don't make me stay.*
Slow down the car
*   I can't keep up*
The pavement is hot
*   and my pads are cut.*
I've got to quit running
*   or my heart will pop*
Every muscle is aching
*   Why didn't you stop?*

I'm so hungry and thirsty
*   darkness is near*
But I shouldn't leave,
*   he will come for me here.*
Several weeks have passed
*   I'm dead on my feet*
They call me a nuisance
*   because I eat off the streets.*
Every car that passes
*   I chase it to see*

If it is my master
    coming for me.

Though I approach
    those that come near
With trust in my eyes
    and no sign of fear
With hate in their voice
    and a cold heartless stare
They threaten to kill me
    they don't even care.
Batter my body
    with rocks that they throw
I will not leave
    he will come, don't they know?

Overtaken by weakness
    my body is numb
I'm sick and so lonely
    oh please, let him come!
I will go back
    to where he first threw me out
I'll wait for him there
    he will come, no doubt.
My thoughts are fading
    my chest feels like lead
I'm sleepy, so sleepy
    I can't lift my head.

It's so quiet so peaceful
    all remains still
There is my master
    at my home on the hill.

Yes, I can see him
  He's calling my name
His voice is so gentle
  His hands are the same.
He decided he wants me
  things will be fine
I really do love him
  that master of mine.

My tail wags with pleasure
  I can't catch my breath.
He came in my dreams…
  but so did my death.

Whisper

TOM MARKSBURY

EDITOR'S NOTE: *"Whisper" is the only story featured in* Circles of Compassion *that departs from the theme of companion animals to depict an interaction with wildlife—in this case a wounded deer. Because it offers an eloquent expression of the feelings experienced by a humane officer during the course of one of the most difficult duties society calls upon such individuals to carry out, it is included.*

THE JOB WAS STILL NEW and exciting; I was trying to get used to working in the daytime after almost six months of night shift. I wasn't used to going to work and finding more than two people in the shelter.

It was an average day; there wasn't all that much going on in my patrol area, the southern part of the county. Just the usual bites and complaints to handle. Then I got a call for an injured deer on Paradise Drive.

I had been on the job for almost six months, and had yet to shoot my first deer. Still anxious about this type of call, I was not looking forward to the experience.

When I arrived at the house, there was no sign of the deer. The driveway was steep and ran downhill from the road. The woman who had called came out of the house to meet me, and gave me what I would come to find out is the usual greeting for this kind of call. "It's over here, it's just awful! I hope there is something you can do for the poor thing!"

She pointed off into the undergrowth just down from her driveway. In a small open spot in the thicket was an adult male deer, a good sized four-point buck. He was lying on the ground looking in my direction.

After suggesting to the woman that she wait in the driveway near my truck, I approached the deer to see what I was dealing with. As I approached, the deer attempted to stand. Both his rear kneecaps were shattered—the legs were attached only by strips of skin and one or two tendons.

I backed away slowly, and the deer settled back down, keeping a very close eye on my movements. I returned to the woman, and told her what I had seen. She asked if there wasn't somewhere I could take the deer to "get better." I told her no, there was no place to take the deer, and I explained that the deer would not appreciate my attempts to move it even if there was a place for me to take it to.

Using the same lines that I had heard other officers use during my training, I tried to explain: the deer would die of stress; the wildlife center could not accept such a badly-injured deer; there was no way to rehabilitate a deer with two broken legs. In training these were easy phrases to pick up. Their true meaning was not yet ingrained.

I advised her that I would have to shoot the deer. She did not take it well. I did my best to console her feelings about the fact I was going to have to shoot this beautiful animal—a symbol of nature's peace and tranquility.

Inside I was in anguish that I would be the one to pull the trigger and kill the deer. She looked at me as someone who does this all the time; the cold, emotionless man in uniform who rids the world of these peaceful, suffering creatures.

Going through the motions, I used the lines that I had picked up along the way: it's what's best for the animal; he is suffering; he won't even hear the gunshot; he'll die immediately. Up to this point I had shot one baby skunk. The bullet tore the entire chest cavity open.

I told her it would be best if she went back into her house. She did, crying. I went back to my truck and got my gun. A Smith and Wesson Model 14, .38 caliber, six-inch barrel, specially modified for target shooting by my soon to be ex-father-in-law.

I got the gun out of the truck and started toward the deer. I had taken no more than two steps with the gun in my hand when the deer stuck up its head, twitched its ears and ran off. I stopped cold in my tracks at the sight of the deer running away. He was headed downhill, running on the stubs of his kneecaps and dragging the flopping bloody forelegs behind. It was a gruesome sight.

I automatically followed as the deer made his way downhill through the brush. I didn't have any trouble keeping track of the deer because of the amount of noise he made charging headlong through the same tangle of underbrush that I could barely struggle through. By the time I got to the bottom of the hillside things had changed. All was quiet. I thought that the deer had stopped right before I emerged from the brush. I was wrong.

The bottom of the hill ended at the shore of San Francisco Bay. There was a small beach that lead into the water. I looked out over the water and could see the deer; he was about 100 yards offshore and swimming out into the bay.

He angled off toward the south of me, now parallel to the shoreline. I followed down the shore, soon discovering that this was not going to be an easy feat. The tide was in, and in places there *was* no shoreline. I had to fight my way through the brush to get past the cliffs that descended directly into the water.

We worked our way south for almost a mile. Most of the time I managed to keep the deer in sight. He stayed several hundred yards offshore. I finally stopped in a small cove to rest. It was a short stretch of beach with cliffs at both ends that extended out into the water. I sat on a rock and looked out to the deer. He was headed into this same stretch of beach.

The rock I was sitting on made good cover. I got down behind it and waited. The deer made his way into the shallow water, out of breath, cold, exhausted. He slowly dragged himself up onto the beach, the small waves from the bay pushing him forward, toward me. The deer was not looking at the beach; his head was hanging down as if the antlers on his head were too heavy to hold up. I waited.

He was almost out of the water. I don't think I had moved even a muscle, but he stopped dead and raised his head to look at me. I can't imagine what was going through his mind. He did not try to get away; he was beyond that.

I brought my gun up to the top of the rock and rested it on my hand. Using the rock to steady the gun I aimed between his eyes. The deer stayed in the same spot and just looked at me. I will never forget the look in those soft brown eyes. I might have been putting my feelings into what I saw, but I don't think so. He seemed to know he was going to die.

I don't think it helped him any but I lowered my gun and whispered to him. I told him that it was okay. He continued looking at me, never moving. We stayed that way for almost five minutes; me whispering every now and then, him looking at me. He never looked at the gun; he only looked into my eyes in a life-and-death game of stare-down. He won, repeatedly. Finally, I ended the game.

It was one of the hardest things I have ever done. I looked beyond the deer to the waters of the bay. No boats in sight. Aim. Breathe. Squeeze. At the very last instant, I closed my eyes.

Bang! I opened my eyes. The deer's head was thrown backwards. He was almost on his back, thrashing in the shallow water. I rushed into the water, grabbed the antlers and turned his head. I placed the muzzle of the pistol against the back of his head and squeezed the trigger. The thrashing stopped. I looked at his face. The brown eyes were dead; no more peace in them. There was a small hole between the eyes, a similar hole in the back of the head. A small amount of blood was seeping out. But very little.

I stood looking out over the water, antler still in one hand, gun in the other. I stood for several minutes, looking for peace on the water. After a time I pulled the deer's body out into the water and pushed it away from the shore. I waded back to the beach and sat on a rock, watching the small waves bouncing against the deer as he moved away from me. The gun was still in my hand, and there was no peace inside me.

We tell ourselves that it is "the best thing to do." Sometimes I can get myself to believe it; other times it is harder. I wish there *was* a magical place that could heal all the animals. The magical place that people believe is out there. I still have my standard lines that I use when I talk to the public, with a better understanding now. But I also carry with me many memories.

Most vivid are the memories of the first animals that I was called upon to "do the best thing for." They all live within me. I will come upon more animals that will need release from suffering, and I will do what needs to be done. And I will do it well, because they need someone who will do it right. The saddest part is that I will also bear the burden of the tears from people who look upon me as a cold unfeeling person who does away with poor innocent animals.

The peace was gone. Only the gun remained. I started back to my truck. As I rounded a point on the shoreline I looked back to the shape in the water. I realized that my life had changed. Could I live with this?

After the long hike I got back to my truck. I was wet, sweaty, full of scratches from the brush and rocky cliffs, and tired. I put the gun away and collapsed on the seat. Closing my eyes, I could still see him looking at me as I aimed just between the eyes.

I was startled by a knock on the window. The woman who made the call. I rolled down the window. She wanted to know what happened. I explained the chase down the hill, over and along the shoreline, and the final outcome on the beach. She turned away crying. "And he fought so hard to live," I heard her sob. Inside me, my life changed again.

I am not the same person I was when I started this job. I have a better understanding of animals. I do what needs to be done, knowing what I know, and understanding that it doesn't really make them feel better…but I still sometimes whisper to them, just before.

Eulogy to Scotty Lightfoot

PAT MILLER

Gallant heart, sightless eyes,
Your suffering is done;
You've faced the demon one last time,
The final battle's won.
Stout of heart, broad of back,
Your journey's been too long;
The world that twice betrayed you
Now will right its wretched wrong.

So you dance away in darkness as you sense her presence near,
And your spotted tendons tremble as you fight against your fear,
Until finally you settle, reassured that we are here,
And trusting in our promise that the way will soon be clear.

Light of heart, fleet of foot,
You'll never want again;
We offer the solution
That will end this life of pain.
Gentle heart, ageless soul,
Go forward from this day;
There is a better place for you,
We send you on your way.

May you gallop on forever over endless emerald fields;
May your footsteps never falter as you wander golden hills;
May your eyes see all the glory that eternity fulfills;
May you know that love surrounds you as your gallant heart stills.

SCOTTY LIGHTFOOT was one of eight horses seized in a Marin County, California neglect case. His owner refused to authorize euthanasia, although the aged Appaloosa was totally blind and suffering from inoperable penile cancer. During the course of the investigation it was discovered that the owner had previously been convicted of horse neglect in another jurisdiction, and that Scotty had been taken away from her then. Somehow, he had fallen back into her hands. Ultimately, the owner was found guilty again, and the judge allowed her one last visit with the horse before his suffering was finally ended.

I Found Your Dog the Other Night

KELLY BUDNER

Hey, I found your dog the other night. Well, I guess "found" is not exactly the right word. It took several of us, on foot and by car, about two hours to track him down. At the end, it was down to just one guy and me. It was Christmas Eve, for heaven's sake. Everyone had something they needed to do—including me. I was just about to give up. We were running out of daylight, it was getting late, and the temperature, which was supposed to drop into the single digits overnight, had already started its downward plummet. Maybe that's why I kept at it. It was a Doberman. I had a Doberman once, and I knew how they hated the cold, and this one already had a strike against him. Even a hundred yards away you could see what an emaciated, pathetic-looking skeleton he was. But he was scared, too, to the point where I didn't know if we could lure him in or not. I had gone to the park that afternoon to walk my own dog before settling in for the evening's festivities. Now, using her and the bag of dog food I always carry in my truck for just such occasions, I was hoping this combination just might do the trick. I could barely pick him out in the fading light when I took my best shot and poured the food on the ground. My dog took her cue and ate with the same religious zeal with which she tackled every meal. It was more than he could bear, and, when he drew closer, I realized that if I couldn't catch him, his chances of getting through this Colorado night were not all that good.

He was a big male, tall at the shoulder, and he should have weighed in at close to 100 pounds. Tonight, he would be lucky to tip the scales at sixty. Every bone in his body knifed through paper-thin skin, and he shook uncontrollably from the cold and from fear. Twice, as I tried to slip a leash over his head, he slashed at my gloved hand with bared teeth. But his obsession with the food was in my favor and, the third time, he never even noticed when the lead settled around his neck. I thought he would fight it, but he didn't.

I took him back to the truck and bid my nameless helper, the one fellow who had stayed on after the others had left, good-bye. He didn't even like Dobermans, he had told me, but, like me, he couldn't walk away from the situation. I put the dog in the front seat and my own slightly miffed female in the back of the truck for the short trip home. I was afraid they might fight otherwise. Actually, it wasn't even my home I was going to, it was my mother's. I was only down for the holidays. You can imagine her elation as I appeared in the midst of guests and holiday prepara- tion with a pony-sized animal that immediately tried to inhale a candy dish full of M&M's when we paused for a moment in the doorway. After that, I kept him confined on blankets in one corner of the house, for his behavior around food, and people, too, was unpredictable, at best. The humane society was closed for the holidays so I had to keep him until Monday. During that time, I fed him every three hours around-the-clock. Too much food at one time and he would inhale it and then throw it back up, so I had to restrict his intake of both food and water at any one time but increase the frequency. He came to know how much time had passed and cried pathetically when the hour drew near. When the food finally hit his system, diarrhea also set in and then he was at the door every two hours. I slept downstairs so I could take him out when he needed to go. On Monday, I fed him all that I could and more and then drove him to the humane society. He slept beside me, still exhausted from his ordeal. When they placed him in a run, I tried not to notice the noble head that stood above the crowd of others yapping and yelping for attention and the eyes that watched as I walked away. He had already started to bond to me, and I to him. Sentiment and reason had wrestled with each other the whole way to the shelter—as they always do. I already had several animals that demanded my personal and financial attention, and I just couldn't take on another one. You can only imagine how much it hurts to come to that same conclusion each time.

I called every couple of days to see how he was getting along. I kept hoping that you were looking for him, that somehow he had just gotten away, and, now that he was somewhere he could be found, you would come searching. One of the guys that helped me the night I found the dog said he had been working in the area the whole day and had seen him running up and down the road since early morning, peering into car windows and then running away. He was looking for you, wasn't he? Even though it was obvious he had been out on his own a lot longer than just one day, he was still looking for you.

I called the morning they put him down, just so I'd know how the story ended. I cried, although I had known all along it was probably going to end up like that. After all, this isn't the first time I've done this. It seems as if people like me are always taking responsibility for the actions of people like you. Happy Holidays.

Isle

DAWN WALLACE

We belong to the Isle of unwanted toys.
We come in great numbers,
All shapes and colors.
Some are brand new,
Some are old and broken,
But all are accepted.

We belong to the Isle of unwanted toys.
We take all comers.
We fix what we can,
We love them one and all.

We belong to the Isle of unwanted toys.
There is no Santa to save us come Christmas Eve,
Only a few to love us…who need and want us.

We belong to the Isle of unwanted toys.
We do what we can,
But we can't do it all.
So we do what we have to,
With love and sadness in our hearts.
We are the Arizona Humane Society.

Fading Masterpieces

KAREN SHEA

THE HINT OF A BREEZE made its way through the window to stir the papers in my hand as I assembled adoption packets. Nearby, Lynn put the finishing touches on a relinquishment form and accepted yet another litter of kittens across the counter. As their former owner pushed open the screen door to leave, he passed our veterinarian, Dr. Chase, who smiled at us and waved. "How's it going?" he asked. We exchanged pleasantries before beginning our work.

Tim, resident canine expert and general shelter "old pro," strode back to the runs to get the dogs in need of vaccinations as Lynn briefed Dr. Chase on the day's proposed agenda. I gathered clipboards and log sheets while preparing myself to deal with the decisions that I'd helped to make that morning. The scenario spun around in my head.

Lynn entered the room as I tossed a soiled litter tray into the trash.

"Any ideas?" she asked. I eyed the yellow paper in her hand and knew without reading its heading what she meant.

"How many?" I inquired.

"We need two cat cages and two kitten cages in these rooms. The other rooms are all set," she said with a sigh. "I've got Muffin and maybe this one," she added. She pointed to a nameless tiger-and-white stray. I nodded in agreement, and we crossed the hall to the kitten room. My eyes scanned the various information cards, avoiding the display of outstretched, velvet paws and the pleading expressions of tiny, whiskered faces.

"Sasha's kittens aren't doing too well," Lynn offered, her solemn voice tinged with uncertainty.

With white underbodies and cloaks of tiger stripes, the kittens bore a striking resemblance to their mother. Curled up together on a crocheted blanket, they slept peacefully.

"They've been kind of sickly all along," I agreed. One of the kittens raised her head, yawned, and blinked sleep from her amber eyes to regard us with a pensive stare.

Lynn scribbled on the yellow paper and surveyed the other cages of kittens. "Look at them all putting on their cute acts."

I hesitated. It had taken a long time to fortify my emotional wall with enough strength to withstand such antics. To my surprise my defenses were pretty strong. I was reluctant to let them weaken. I forced myself to look at the reaching paws and desperate young faces pressed to the bars, but they elicited little emotion. My wall allowed me to keep anthropomorphism at bay too. These were not kittens pleading with us for another day, another chance at life. They couldn't possibly understand the gravity of our business.

I was shaken; had I become incapable of feeling? With a deep breath, I quickly swept the thought from my head. My eyes scanned the cages several times, always pausing at the same one. Picasso, named for the seemingly arbitrary spattering of black and orange patches on her otherwise white coat, pressed her neck and shoulder along the metal bars as if trying to break them with the force of her affection.

She had been through a great deal—fleas, intestinal parasites, a respiratory infection, and anemia—in just four short months of life. Though she responded well to treatment, she still wasn't in the best of health. Life as a stray, dumped in a remote field of a rural town to fend for herself was no way to start out in life.

The fact that everyone had grown attached to Picasso had already bought her several extra weeks. The precious fragments of time that we collected and spent with her made her special to us, but that very element which made her unique could also snatch her away from us forever. Time is a tricky notion. Intangible, yet indispensable, it is ever in short supply, especially in animal shelters. Space limitations further complicate the process of juggling lives (for that is often what we seem to be doing). No animal can stay indefinitely. It would be unfair. Every day there are five, maybe ten more who deserve an equal chance. All of these factors made Picasso the most likely nominee to be placed on the list.

Picasso's trilling snapped me out of my reverie. Logic told me she should be next on the list, but my heart pleaded for some kind of justice.

Lynn pressed a finger to her mouth and chewed her lip in silence. She was waiting for a cue from me, but I knew that my next words could be a death sentence. She was the first to speak.

"I hate to see Picasso go. She is so sweet, but we've given her every chance. God, look at her."

Picasso sat with a paw gently curved around the unyielding metal bars, her head tilted slightly to one side as if in question. A section of my wall crumbled. I looked away.

In a voice weakened by a deluge of emotions, I admitted, "I was thinking the same thing; I just didn't want to say it."

The click of toenails echoed in the hall. Tim entered with a dog, and vaccinations got under way. Things moved along relatively uneventfully as a few dogs and nearly a dozen cats were examined. Dr. Chase looked at his watch. "How many euthanasias do we have scheduled for today?" he asked.

I scanned the list. "One dog, nine cats." The detached tone of my voice reverberated in my ears.

"We'd better get started."

Dogs are usually first. They are more predictable. A bloated terrier-mix lacking much of its wiry, gray hair was led in and placed on the table. Tim persuaded her to sit.

I recognized her immediately. She had been picked up as a stray in a public housing complex that didn't allow pets. Perhaps her original owner had moved and left her in the care of his neighbors without informing them. She had become "public property," receiving plentiful handouts from people with good intentions, but no one was willing to do more than feed her. What about medical care, shelter, or love? It was "someone else's" responsibility, but "someone else" is a mere fictional entity created by people to quiet their own conscience.

"Hmm," Dr. Chase said as if to himself. "Cushingoid belly," he added.

"What?!" Tim and I asked in unison.

"Cushing's Disease. It's a hormone imbalance—accounts for the hair loss too," he explained as he slipped the needle into a vein in her foreleg. "It's usually caused by a tumor or other abnormality of the adrenal gland." We nodded solemnly, saddened by the circumstances under which we were receiving our lesson in veterinary medicine.

Tim gently scratched the dog's ear as he looked stonily at the site of the injection, ready to keep any flinch or struggle in check.

Tim supported the dog's body as she slumped against him. She slid slowly, quietly to her side. Her now useless legs hung awkwardly over the table's edge. The balding mound of her belly gradually ceased its rhythmic rise and fall.

Her eyes remained open, windows into the unknown. Perhaps that is why death never looks quite like sleep.

It is an odd thing to be present and a part of the moment

linking life and death. I always feel tempted to challenge the irreversible. There was a sense of urgency to regain that which was just there before my eyes, that which was gone through some terrible wrong. Seconds before, this dog had walked into the room by her own power, the magnificent mystery called life. Now she is nothing more than fuel for the crematory. What if...? Then I was at the edge of the table grasping a stiff plastic bag. Tim slid her body, now a gray blur, off the table and into the bag. There was an explosion of sound as inanimate flesh landed against plastic. My hands tightened around the bag's wrinkled edges to keep the limpness from crashing to the floor. I didn't want to hear the thud of her tender body hitting the linoleum.

Tim took the bag and placed it gently aside. I recorded the dog's passing with a series of sterile numbers and codes. Her name was Fluffy.

The smell of bleach engulfed the room as I cleaned the table. Lynn entered with Sasha's kittens. She handed one to Dr. Chase and one to me. The kitten proceeded to scale my shirt in search of a more suitable perch. As her sister died not five feet away, I occupied myself by redirecting the path of her needle-sharp claws and thought, "If there is one inevitable truth in the world, it is this: An unspayed cat allowed to roam will, without fail, produce a number of kittens far greater than the number of available homes." It ranks up there with the Law of Gravity.

Before I knew it, it was her turn. I was overcome momentarily with guilt as she clung tightly to me. Did she understand what was going to happen? Was she asking that I protect her? "Anthropomorphism," I reminded myself, and unhooked her claws from my shirt.

Kittens veins are tiny. Dr. Chase gently grasped her by the scruff of the neck and raised her from the table to face him. Her legs flailed about in the air (perhaps seeking my shirt?) Dr. Chase dodged the kitchen's unsheathed claws to deliver the syringe's fatal contents. She cried out. Was it a scream of pain, or fear, or protest? Her legs slowed their frantic motion and finally drooped silently with the weight of death.

Picasso was next. The tightening in my throat was followed by a nagging ache in my heart. I fought tears as Lynn entered with Picasso cradled in her arms.

Picasso cried in protest as her graceful feline form was manipulated into what seemed like an embarrassingly awkward position. She didn't like this kind of game. She wanted to run free, nap on sunny window sills, chase killer dust bunnies. Her cries increased in volume as she tried to squirm free. Dr. Chase searched for the proper spot with skilled hands and the beveled tip of a needle.

No, this was not a game. It was something strange and evil. Picasso's howling escalated with the continuing struggle. Desperately, she challenged the hand that grasped the skin behind her neck. She strained to arch her back and swing her head around, teeth bared and ready to spear the enemy.

I wanted to shout, "Wait! Stop! Someone will adopt her tomorrow, next week, someday"—but my throat was too constricted for the words to pass. Yowls emerged from the very depths of Picasso's young being. They seemed to last an eternity. The scene before me blurred behind a watery curtain.

Dr. Chase found his mark. As the brilliant blue liquid from the syringe began to take effect, the intensity of Picasso's screams dwindled. There was no last minute rescue, no "happily ever after" ending for her. Her cries ceased and the brilliant hues from her sleek coat seemed to fade before my eyes.

Lynn curled Picasso's lifeless body into a graceful arc, the position in which she had so often slept. But it wasn't sleep. Her eyes were full of nothingness and her tiny mouth was ajar, silenced in mid-cry.

The rest of the day's euthanasias were a blur for me. Sometime toward the end, without warning, one of the plastic bags in the corner of the room heaved laboriously and emitted a high-pitched sigh. We all stared at it, our eyes filled horror. Wasn't the animal dead? Of course. It was just the lungs, retiring from their lifelong duty, expelling a final weary breath. We looked at each other and laughed. It was not the laughter of amusement, but the laughter of unshed tears overflowing.

Pigeons

PAT MILLER

"I'm getting too old," the owner said,
"to care for them anymore."
And my heart grew heavy and cold with dread,
for I knew just what was in store.

"They're only pigeons," I heard someone say
as the owner walked out the door.
But he wasn't in the back room that day
as the bodies piled up on the floor.

With satin soft feathers beneath our hands,
feeling tiny hearts pounding from fright,
the burden of our job's unfair demands
weighed heavy on us that night.

One by one we held them close
as we asked each other why.
One by one we injected the dose
that would cause each pigeon to die.

One by one those hearts were stilled
'til one hundred and ten lay dead,
one by one the birds were killed
'til the silence rang loud in our heads.

Did you hear the flutter of one hundred ten
pairs of wings that day?
Or was it the sound of a hundred ten souls
silently slipping away?

PART II

THE MAKING
OF ALLIANCES

When we have grasped the great central fact
about animals, that they are in the full sense our
fellow-beings, all else will follow for them.

HENRY SALT (1851-1939)

Pippin

JEANIE ROBINSON-POWNALL

PIPPIN (pip' in) noun. 1. A variety of apple. 2. A term of endearment for a small child. 3. A person or thing much admired.

I FOUND HER IN THE BARN. The barn had seen better days; it was tumbledown with gaping holes in the roof that let in the elements. This was actually a good thing because apples fell in through one of the holes and landed in the cow manure. Her chain was four feet long, and by really straining she could reach the apples. She had no collar, and the prongs that attached the clasp to the chain gouged and tore at her neck when she pulled and strained toward the apples. Her neck was raw and rank with infection. I could see there was one apple, tantalizingly out of reach. The blood dripping from her neck showed how hard she had tried to reach it to slake her thirst and hunger.

She greeted me joyously, with the frenzied enthusiasm of a captive greeting her liberator. My heart sank when I smelled the vile mingling of odors: her waste, which she could not quite get out of; the infection of her neck, which dripped pus down her legs and onto the ground; and the cow manure produced from the relatively healthy calf sharing a section of the barn with her.

I had seen thin animals before, but never had I seen a dog this thin. Not only did every rib stand out, but the skin sunk down between each rib. She was a skeleton covered by skin and fur with a pitiful sunken-in face. Yet she had spirit.

As I bent down to examine her neck, unaware of what the other end of her was doing, her tail swept a pile of cow manure right down the front of my V-neck shirt. It came to rest in my bra. It was then that I noticed reddish splotches were appearing on my clothing. It was blood, pumped from a gaping wound on her tail. Beneath the blood, white bone glistened.

The veterinarian wasn't sure he could save her—she was emaciated and her neck was gangrenous. Yet her spirit impressed him, as did the trusting brown eyes, huge in her sunken face. "We'll try," was all he would promise.

He tried and so did she, and when I brought her home she sat in front of the couch, directly on my feet, and gently accepted popcorn from my fingers. That night I let her up on the bed; how could I make her sleep on the floor with all those bones poking through her skin? The vet agreed to spay her once she'd doubled her weight. She weighed nineteen pounds when I brought her home from the hospital; she weighed forty-seven pounds in her prime. She always liked apples, and ate my apple cores with relish.

She and I were a pair through the rest of my unmarried years. I kept her impeccably clean and brushed, and enjoyed taking my very friendly, very beautiful, very glossy black dog with the very big feet everywhere with me. I married, had two children, and grew into early middle age while she grew old. During her last year on this earth she saved our two-year-old son's life. On a sub-zero night, while he was headed on his merry way out the front door while the rest of us slept, she positioned herself under our bedroom door and howled. Pretty remarkable, considering she'd been deaf for two years.

After fourteen years of stewardship (she in mine and I in hers), we laid her to rest in the backyard, under the trees where she'd spent much of her twilight years sleeping. The daffodils on her grave bloom every spring, and our children's little sneakered-feet have beaten a path around her resting place. She lived a life that was dominated by good nature, valor, and sweetness. She was adaptable, well-mannered, and got along well with everyone she met. I hope when my time comes I deserve such an epitaph, but I am sure I will fall far short of Pippin.

PIPPIN WAS THE SUBJECT of Jeanie Robinson-Pownall's first cruelty investigation for the Allegheny County SPCA. After her rescue and adoption by the author, she contributed to the organization's educational and fundraising efforts by serving as a mascot and helping staff their informational booth at county fairs and other events.

Guarded but Hopeful

DIANA B. TIDD

THE HUMANE SOCIETY of Southeast Missouri is a fairly young organization, having been incorporated in 1978. In its short life, the group has faced many uphill battles and struggles for survival. But the spring of 1991 was one of the toughest times our organization had ever faced.

Due to many factors—including a lack of funds, stress and burn-out among staff and volunteers, an overwhelming demand for services, and all the "routine" challenges that face animal shelters nationwide, we found ourselves in crisis. Our future was at best uncertain unless we could come up with a way to reorganize and revitalize the organization. In the process of trying to meet these challenges, the shelter was hit by a devastating blow—a severe outbreak of parvovirus hit our kennels. Parvovirus is almost always fatal, and it is highly contagious. The veterinarians who worked with us advised us that the only way to contain the disease would be to put down the *entire* canine population in the shelter. The only exceptions would be animals with a known medical background and vaccination history. Since a large percentage of the animals our shelter takes in are strays, this meant practically all the puppies and adult dogs we had would be euthanized, and new ones coming in would have to be put down as soon as their legal holding period was up. This would be the only way to insure that the kennels could be completely disinfected and sterilized.

Even though an event of this nature is rare, when it does happen it is devastating.

Betsy, a fellow member of the board of directors, and I had come in to see if we could be of any help. Only one staff member, Chad, and one volunteer were on hand. The shelter was eerily quiet. Even the cats, unaffected by the epidemic, were silent. Chad, who had just been in the euthanasia room (a room in which he had spent entirely too much time in the last two days), greeted us in the front office. He was showing the strain of the awful job he was having to do.

We were all talking, trying to understand how we were going to weather this awful ordeal, when one of the animal control officers for the City of Cape Girardeau came in, his outstretched arms gingerly carrying a small animal. At first we thought it might be a young possum; it was hard to tell. The poor little creature had absolutely no hair and his body was encrusted with open sores and scabs. The animal control officer explained it was a puppy that had appeared at the home of a couple a few days before. The couple had tried unsuccessfully to treat the pup at home for what they thought was a *flea* infestation. When their efforts proved futile (and probably actually did additional harm to the puppy's sensitive skin), and no owner could be found, they had called the city to have him picked up.

Chad knew that in keeping with our veterinarian's advice, there was no choice. Not only was this puppy's medical background unknown, and the likelihood of him having received proper vaccinations poor, but he was in desperate condition. Chad left the room to prepare a syringe.

While Chad was gone, Betsy draped a towel around the bald puppy and held him close. I watched him gaze up into her eyes with such trust that it was as if he knew she would protect him. Chad returned to collect the puppy for the trip back to the euthanasia room. As he reached out to take the pup, Betsy declared, "No! Not this one! After all he's been through, he's going to get a second chance."

We took the puppy to a long-time supporter of the shelter, Dr. Freitag. She admitted him to her hospital, diagnosed his condition as severe demodectic mange (a disease common in puppies whose mothers have suffered from poor nutrition or in litters born or raised in unsanitary conditions), and began treatment. The prognosis was guarded but hopeful.

In the meantime, the effort to improve the shelter's health and to insure its survival began. Every few days though, we would get an update on "Puppy," as he came to be called. He improved daily, and it appeared he would indeed have that second chance Betsy had promised. For the next two months, the work went forward. The board struggled to make the shelter healthy, and "Puppy" worked hard to get well and prepare himself to be placed in a permanent home.

The story has a happy ending—or perhaps more appropriately, a new beginning. In July of 1991 a dedicated, bright and compassionate young woman gave our organization a new beginning by becoming the shelter's new administrator. Not too long after she embarked on the tremendous task of revitalizing our organization and guiding it into the future, she met "Puppy," who by now had come to embody just what all of us were doing and why. This beautiful, silky, black long-haired youngster with the sparkling eyes and dancing tail was virtually unrecognizable as the poor sickly little pup who had come to us just a few months before during such desperate times. In a tongue-in-cheek gesture, our friend had been dubbed with the nickname "Mange Mutt" during his long recovery period. Never had an animal been more inappropriately labeled! By the time he was ready to be put up for adoption though, his name had stuck. The name made little difference though. Our new administrator took one look at our Mange Mutt and fell in love. Our friend had found his home.

Mange Mutt comes to visit the shelter regularly. He knows no such thing as a stranger, he loves everyone he meets and he takes for granted that everyone loves him back. We all do; it's impossible not to. It is as if he knows how close to death he came and he relishes every second of his life and adores all those who cross his path. In addition to sharing his home with the cats and other dogs that make up his permanent family, he also helps in the foster care of sick and injured animals. Most importantly though, Mange Mutt helps us to remember, when we become discouraged, that we do make a difference. One look at that face and those adoring brown eyes and it's possible to keep going.

The Laska Chronicles

JULIE ANN MOCK

THE SUMMER OF 1993 wasn't much different from previous summers at the shelter: too many cats, too many kittens, and a constant struggle to accommodate and care for them all. Unlike most people, those of us who work or volunteer in animal shelters are never glad to see spring and summer come. There is an official mourning period in early March when we say goodbye to the low numbers of shelter residents typical during winter. A small population affords time for individualized care and the opportunity to take on creative projects to improve shelter life for the animals. Once spring arrives, so do kittens and a lot more cats.

Laska came to us during the first days of summer when the shelter was teeming with kittens and other adults. My volunteer job involves a variety of duties, including cleaning cages, giving medications, and helping with treatments in Sick Bay. Working with the cats in the Sick Bay provides an opportunity to get to know the ailing animals, but it leaves little chance to get to know the animals who are in the adoption area. Even so, I noticed Laska. She was a striking long-haired tortoise-shell patterned cat with white patches. She had been brought into the shelter by neighbors who said that her owners had moved and left her behind.

If I had known then what would eventually transpire, I would have paid better attention. But summers at the shelter are so busy time tends to rush by in a blur. I do remember observing Laska. She appeared to be a fairly large cat, very pretty and very proud, but rather reserved. I remember thinking to myself that she must have known she had been abandoned. She seemed hesitant to accept the modest comforts of shelter life and the attention of volunteers. I remember taking her out of her cage once or twice and holding her in my lap. She was polite and perhaps even purred a bit, but she still seemed detached.

It was when she stopped eating that I started to notice her more. She was put in Sick Bay with the hope that some fluids and extra attention would bring her around. When it comes to winning over frightened or depressed cats, we volunteers are a determined lot. We never say never. No matter how frightened or shy a cat may be initially, with enough patience and love we are almost always able to eventually elicit trusting purrs and nudges.

Neither the fluids nor the extra attention seemed to be getting the desired results with Laska though. She continued losing weight, and her food remained untouched. We pressed on though, certain that like so many others before her, she would respond.

It was around this time that I was scheduled to take ten days off from shelter duties to help with a fundraising event for our volunteer program. With little experience in putting on such an event, I became consumed with the task at hand. I'm ashamed to say that during my time away from the shelter, I never once thought about Laska.

When I returned to work though, I learned that her condition had deteriorated to the point where the shelter veterinarian was recommending euthanasia. Too weak to stand, and incontinent, Laska was a heartbreaking sight to see. With any other cat in such poor condition, I would have supported the decision that immediate euthanasia was the only choice and that the animal's suffering should be ended. But with Laska something was different. I couldn't stand the thought of losing her without ever knowing why she had stopped eating. There had to be a reason. Unless she was afflicted with a deadly disease, wasn't there *something* that could be done for her?

I remember taking her to the veterinarian in the bottom half of a plastic travel kennel. After years of witnessing first-hand the amazing speed, agility, and Houdini-like escape capabilities of most cats, it was a strange experience to have a cat in my car who wouldn't—indeed couldn't—go anywhere.

I brought Laska to work with me the next day to await the results of the blood panel. She was so near death that unless an answer could be found and some kind of treatment initiated, she would have to be euthanized. While I worked that morning, she lay silently in her carrier "bed," with officers and staff stopping by to offer a kind word or a pat on the head. When the time finally came to make the call to the veterinarian, I was nervous, yet resigned. The tests would tell us the right—though potentially heartbreaking—thing to do.

The blood work revealed only acute anemia, which was an obvious result of anorexia. The veterinarian prescribed an intensive course of syringe feeding, and some blood fortifying drugs and other medications, all of which might or might not save her. He wasn't willing to give up on her yet though, and neither was I.

My husband and I have an agreement which I grudgingly admit is fair: with all the time I spend at the shelter, our own very complete animal family, lots of travel, and a busy social schedule, I don't bring home foster animals. Exceptions to this have been rare, but when they have occurred they have been very temporary and their terms have been iron-clad. So, what to do? When all else failed, I opted for denial. These were my rationales: Though I wanted to believe otherwise, I was afraid Laska probably wasn't going to make it; we didn't have to worry about her disrupting our house, escaping or upsetting our own cats—she was too weak; and she would only stay with us until she started eating. The last item turned out to be the most laughable. Would I really have taken her back to the shelter where she had done so poorly—where her total food consumption could have fit on the head of a pin, and left room to spare?

The news that I was fostering Laska at my house was met with relief and expressions of joy and support from the other volunteers. When they hadn't seen her, they had feared she had been put down. Karen offered to help with her care if we had to go away, and Cindy offered the greatest of gifts—a potential home if Laska recovered. All of this assumed her survival.

Progress with Laska was slow, but it was steady. The veterinarian had warned that her recovery could take months and would require intensive care. At six pounds, she'd lost about half her body weight. One day as I combed some stray food from under her chin, a large patch of fur pulled loose! She was completely helpless. But she had only been with us a few days when it became clear that I was not to be her only nurse. Our shelter-adopted cat Melanie, a mother before she had come to us and been spayed, displayed all her maternal skills with Laska. She demanded to see her foundling, and with Laska's permission, was welcomed onto the rehabilitation team. Hygiene is Melanie's specialty, and I'm certain that the once proud and immaculate Laska found comfort in her new friend's grooming services.

After ten days Laska started using a litter box placed near her bed. After three weeks of syringe feeding, she took her first bites of solid food. All the while, she was cheered on by friends who celebrated each small step as a major victory. These were my kind of people, who welcomed a phone call at ten at night to hear about Laska's first litter box trek, or who would stop by at feeding time just to watch Laska eat. Karen even brought warm baked chicken breasts to share with Laska.

When she started eating and moving around more easily, I

brought her downstairs so she wouldn't be lonely. From her behavior at the shelter, I would not have expected Laska would be especially compatible with other cats, but she proved me wrong. Her manner was completely calm and non-threatening, even when my grumpiest male cat hissed in her face! As Laska's recovery progressed, she and Melanie took to conducting mutual grooming sessions. Afterwards they could often be seen sleeping together, sharing the same patch of morning sun.

Cindy's home was still available and Laska was quickly approaching the point at which she'd be ready for adoption. Meanwhile, my husband and I, who had no intention of keeping her, were fighting a losing battle against a cat with a story, and perhaps even a plan. Looking back, it seems as if it was inevitable. We were headed for the point of no return from day one. I was able to fool myself with the notion that the situation was temporary because Laska would have a home when she was ready. But Laska knew better. The cat who was reserved and elusive to so many made a brazen play for my husband and charmed all our other animals into submission. Most importantly though, Laska *made* it. Hers was a story we loved being a part of, and once it was clear she had made it, we didn't want to let her go.

So Laska lives with us. We have had her for almost seven months now, in which time her coat has grown soft and shiny, she has gained two more pounds, and she has become a fairly good eater. In many ways she is still a mystery to us, bearing little resemblance to the gopher-hunting wonder the people who turned her in reported. She is sweet, has impeccable house manners, and gets along with everyone. Melanie, self-appointed feline social director of our household, would like to make a playmate out of Laska, but it remains to be seen if Laska, still recovering and not yet very active, will comply.

Laska likes to lick our hands and faces, purrs a lot, loves blankets, hates tile, and often sneaks into our bed at night to sleep between us. She gets fed whenever she wants, whatever she wants, wherever she wants (wouldn't you know, she prefers to eat on carpet)! She maintains a whole team of cheerleaders ready to enjoy every chase of the tail and pretty pose.

All I want to know is, who writes these scripts? We can only laugh now about the unusual events which conspired to bring Laska to us. Whose design was it that a cat from outside the shelter's normal jurisdiction made her way to us, came very close to being euthanized but wasn't, wasn't given much chance of surviving but did, was taken into a foster home where foster animals weren't normally taken, and was adopted into that same home by people who had sworn that their animal family was large enough? My husband, always the pragmatist, is more than willing to blame at least the last three of these on me, but I know no mere mortal like myself could come close to creating such a scenario. One of my favorite songs asks, "Do you believe in fairy tales? Can love survive when all else fails?" You bet!

Gable the Cat

MICHELLE LAROUX

There once was a woman
*   who lived all alone,*
Her husband had died,
*   and her home had grown,*
Cold and lonely with nobody there,
To talk to, or eat with, and his empty chair
Made her feel so abandoned
*   and full of despair.*

Until one day at the table she sat,
And she thought to herself
*   what I need is a cat.*
So she drove to the Shelter
*   to see what was there,*
She took a deep breath
*   and said a quick prayer,*
Walked in the cat room fully prepared.

She planned to take home a cat,
*   but what she didn't know,*
Was how many there'd be,
*   and such tales of woe.*
How could she decide on one of these cats,
Should she take that one, shiny and black,
Or the orange tabby so quiet and fat.

One seemed half frozen,
   one hid in a sack,
One's name was Pushkin,
   another was Mack.
Then she saw one named Gable,
   he looked rather ill,
And she watched as the caretaker
   gave him a pill,
Then he lay in the corner of his cage,
   very still.

She went up to his cage
   and she whispered his name,
He meowed from the corner,
   and up he came.
To the door of the cage,
   and he reached out a paw,
It was then, when she opened the door
   that she saw,
Bald patches of skin
   and a spot that was raw.

She thought to herself, this kitty is sick,
And just then Gable gave her a lick,
On her finger that was holding the door,
He purred and he rubbed up
   against her for more,
Little did he know what she had in store.

For she filled out the papers
   and gave him a pat,
Then she whispered again
   to the sickly gray cat,

"I'll be back for you honey,
    just you wait and see!"
Then she hustled and bustled
    about like a bee,
Getting things ready for her kitty cat.

She bought him some food,
    a bed, and a rat,
A toy rat, of course,
    and a post he could scratch.
You see, she and Gable
    were the purrfect match,
For his heart and her heart
    were firmly attached!

She treated his skin
    and she fattened him up,
She let him sip milk
    from an old antique cup.
She watched him get healthy
    and stronger each day,
His fur became thick and a beautiful gray,
And now his eyes twinkled
    and he loved to play.

And he sat with the woman,
    curled up on her lap,
Everyday about two
    when he took his cat nap.
And the lady was no longer lonely or upset,
She had Gable the cat,
    all she'd needed was a pet.

Faith and a Dog Named Max

MIKE ROWELL

A T THE SANTA BARBARA Buddhist Priory, there's a dog named Max who's living testament to the belief that with a little faith and a lot of support, any animal can achieve his or her full potential.

One rainy afternoon as San Francisco SPCA Education Coordinator Judy Jenkins returned to her office from lunch, she caught sight of a frightened and scruffy black-and-white dog roaming the parking lot. Judy tried to lure him into the building with remnants of her lunch, but the dog, paralyzed with fear, backed himself into a corner and refused to respond.

Eventually, with the help of some volunteers, Max, as he came to be called, was coaxed into the shelter. He didn't appear to be starved, but he was dirty, matted and unkempt. Judy guessed that he had lived in someone's backyard—probably someone who had taken little care of him and eventually abandoned him to the streets.

Judy immediately became attached to this canine castaway with the fuzzy coat and suspicious eyes. A veterinary examination at the shelter revealed that the approximately one-year-old Max was in sound physical shape, but emotionally he was hurting, probably due to neglect and mistreatment by humans. Max was terrified of people, especially men. Whenever a man came near Max, the diffident dog would put his tail between his legs, try to hide, and bark fearfully.

Max's behavior problem led Judy to fear that few people would want to adopt him. So one week after Max came to the shelter and no one had claimed him as their missing stray, Judy took him home.

At first, Max was as fearful of Judy as he was of other humans. Luckily, Judy had a diplomat to act on her behalf: her Golden Retriever, Chelsea. Somewhere along the way, Max must have learned to trust dogs in a way he didn't trust people. In no time at all he bonded to Chelsea and began taking lessons from her on living in the world of humans. Slowly, by following Chelsea's example, Max learned that at least one human—Judy—was worthy of his trust.

For the first month Max was too scared to even be trained or to withstand a visit to the veterinarian for neutering. But he was slowly responding to Judy's patience, attention, and love as well as Chelsea's efforts, and by the second month Judy was able to house-train Max and bring him to the shelter's clinic for neutering. Yet even as Max was becoming less reluctant with Judy, he remained terrified of other people. So Judy decided his next step in becoming more trusting would be to go to work with her every day as Chelsea did. But as Max tried to fit in at work, new problems emerged. He became increasingly protective of Judy's desk, viewing it as solely his and Judy's territory. And when men approached Judy's office, Max would once again become fright-ened and anxious.

Everyone who knew Judy soon knew Max. Many people dis-missed Max as a lost cause. They said a dog like Max couldn't be trusted, that sooner or later he would get scared and bite someone. Judy ignored these ominous warnings; she knew that all Max needed was an intense "re-training course" in human relations. He had to unlearn all the fearful behavior patterns he had learned during his first years of life, and he needed a chance to gain trust in humankind, especially men. To accomplish this, Judy felt Max needed not just a man in his life, but a very special man, who would be understanding and would love Max enough to see him through.

So Judy put out the word that she was looking for just such a special home for Max. It was not easy trying to convince people it was possible to rebuild the dog's faith in humans. Even when Judy placed an ad in the paper, the person taking the classifieds information told her she ought to have the dog put to sleep!

But Judy would not give up. She told Max's story to anyone and everyone who would listen. She even called the monks of a Buddhist priory where she had previously placed some former laboratory rats. The monks passed Judy's appeal on to other priories, and Max's tale eventually reached the Reverend Jisho Perry, the man in charge of the Buddhist Priory in Santa Barbara, California.

When Perry called to make arrangements to meet Max, Judy felt conflicting emotions. On one hand, she was glad that her hopes for a loving home for Max might become a reality. But she was also saddened by the prospect of saying goodbye to her friend of four months. She realized, though, that Max's needs took precedence over her own. She made arrangements with Perry to see Max.

When Perry arrived, Max was—as usual—scared, but not as frightened as he had been around other men. Something was different about this man. This soft-spoken monk wore robes and acted in a gentle manner. Still, Perry had to bribe Max with a treat to get close enough to pet him. Chelsea pitched in by demonstrating approval of Perry. By the end of the visit, Max seemed more at ease. Perry decided to take Max home to the priory. As Max left, somewhat frightened and confused, he looked back longingly at Judy; as Judy watched the robed man leave with Max, she fought back tears. Was she doing the right thing?

Things did not improve right away when the pair arrived back in Santa Barbara. Max was too scared to even relieve himself, and spent most of his first two weeks hiding under the furniture. When he finally gained enough confidence to come out from his hiding place, Perry discovered that Max was extremely sensitive about being touched. Max was indeed a tough case.

But none of this deterred Perry. Like Judy, he believed in Max. Perry simply refused to take the dog's fears too seriously. Instead, the monk spent much of his time just being with Max, letting the dog find out for himself that life with people could feel safe after all. Slowly, Max's emotional scars began to heal.

Meditation time at the priory proved to be a perfect opportunity for Max. Here was a whole group of people who, for half an hour at a time, would sit absolutely still—and in complete silence. Max discovered he could walk up to them and sniff and no one would react. In Max's experience, this was surely an extraordinary phenomenon. Here he was able to investigate humans without the slightest fear of being struck or yelled at—in fact, without so much as a glance of disapproval. Max learned.

As Max's fears gave way to trust, Perry began working with him on obedience training. Max caught on. Once, Max went out of his way to prove how well-mannered he was. Perry had taught him to first sit and then listen for the "OK" before being allowed to eat. One afternoon, Perry set down Max's food and the dog obediently sat, but just then some guests were leaving and Perry left the kitchen to say goodbye to them. Instead of gobbling his food, Max trotted out to the front door and made a point of sitting in front of everyone so they could see he was still waiting for his signal.

After more than a year of working with Max and training him, Perry had Max certified as an official therapy dog. To receive certification, Max had to show that he was obedient, reliable, of sound temperament and friendly with people and other animals.

Max??

Max now visits schools and health care institutions, acting as an unabashed ambassador of goodwill. "If I walk down the hall, no one notices," Perry says. "If I walk down the hall with Max, everyone comes out, eager to meet Max." And lo and behold, Max is eager to greet them too.

It's been nearly three years since Judy Jenkins rescued the terrified stray from the shelter's parking lot. The dog who feared all humans now greets groups of twenty or thirty people with ease. The dog who loathed being touched now lets youngsters give him baths and brush him. And the dog that growled at men is now a man's constant companion.

"He's a fun dog to be with," says Perry. "Everyone's been good to him, teaching him that people can be trusted." Now the Priory's official Public Relations Officer, Max acts as a calming influence on visitors and likes nothing better than being the center of attention. He consoles people when they're "down" and counsels them when they need a friend, demonstrating remarkable intuition for a dog who once wanted nothing to do with people.

Max has proven his spirit's ability to conquer all his past setbacks. The dog is an example of potential fulfilled for everyone who visits the priory, and Perry is glad to see that one of his motivations in adopting Max has come to fruition: "I liked the idea of adopting a dog who had otherwise had a very rough time of it... and giving him a chance to trust and help others."

Max has proven that, given the chance, any animal's spirit can come through. All it takes is someone with a little patience, persistence and gentleness. And a little faith.

Grandma

GARY DUNGAN

S HE WAS AN OLD apple-headed Siamese, the kind that typified the breed before someone decided that Siamese cats should like more like Collie dogs than cats. She was from what a breeder would have called "questionable lineage." Actually, she was an alley cat—literally. She was found wandering around downtown Denver, Colorado. She was thin, wary of strangers, and very pregnant. An elderly woman had brought her home and called the animal shelter where I worked, begging us to pick her up. Although we didn't normally pick up stray cats, it was on my way home from work (more or less), so I volunteered to do it.

She was indeed quite pregnant, and emaciated. Her coat looked more like brown straw than fur. And she definitely was not fond of strange people or car rides. She yowled incessantly the entire way home. It wasn't that she was frightened—she just seemed mad about being inconvenienced.

I kept her at home. I knew that in her condition, she was not a likely candidate for adoption, and the first impression she imparted was not very favorable. I wondered if she hadn't been trained as a "guard cat" at some point in her life.

She ate as if another meal would never be served. After about a week she gave birth to nine kittens, all of which mirrored their mother's malnourished condition. All the kittens were euthanized, for their survival was unlikely and her ability to sustain them poor. After giving birth to the kittens, her condition improved dramatically. She did have ringworm, but it was a treatable problem. She was cured after about eight weeks, but not before she had managed to pass the condition on to me!

She was convinced that the perfect place in life was my lap, particularly at night when I watched TV or read. Once situated, she would become enormously annoyed at what she perceived to be any unnecessary movement. Heaven forbid one should ever consider intentionally disturbing her. If I moved her from my lap at a moment she did not approve of, she would turn around and bite me! It was as if she was saying to me, "how *dare* you forget who is in charge in our relationship!"

Strangers were her special prey. I remember too many times when someone new would come to the house, sit down, and immediately be greeted by a seemingly friendly and unassuming Siamese cat rubbing against their leg. As they would reach down to pet her—a perfectly normal thing to do—the unsuspecting stranger's hand would be met with a sharp bite. She took great pleasure in this maneuver, sauntering off to the bedroom afterwards, joyful that she had taught one more human who was "boss."

My household in those days was teeming with creatures, many of them animals with special needs from the shelter where I worked. Dogs and cats who were sick, puppies and kittens who were too young for adoption and needed foster care, and other animals that needed a little extra TLC found their way into my home. My feline friend put up with all of these intruders with circumspect disgust. Dogs—especially puppies—were only tolerated *after* they had been suitably disciplined with unsheathed claws to the nose and a very loud hiss.

Adult cats were similarly received—with ears flat, claws out and that inimitable yowl of hers. Kittens though were an entirely different story. She treated every kitten as if it were her own; the kittens reciprocated as if she were their kin. She was a doting foster mother, spending much of her time grooming her orphans, and when necessary, doling out discipline if one of her charges stepped out of line. She could often be seen moving them about, one by one, by the scruff of the neck if their location did not suit her.

We named her Amanda Cat originally, but her advanced age and doting nature with kittens, led us to call her, simply, Grandma. The name stuck. By our best guess, she was about twelve. For most if not all of those years she had probably been an outside cat. Her transition to life as an indoor cat with us was often a battle; when she did get out though she didn't seem interested in going far. Usually we'd find her laying in the shade of an enormous cedar bush in front of our house. She became resigned and ultimately, I believe, content being an indoor cat.

Nothing is ever certain in life, and when separation and divorce intervened in my life, old Grandma cat came with me. Moving did not sit well with her, but as with most other things in her life, she adjusted, though not without a good deal of grumbling. Through all the trying times and changes, Grandma was a true companion, always willing—in fact demanding—to sit on my lap and purr, and always willing to bite me if my conduct was not consistent with her wishes!

Even after a traumatic move some thousand miles to Arizona, to a climate that must have seemed strange to her after a lifetime in Colorado, she remained, until the end, irascible. But age began to take its toll on old Grandma Cat, as it does too often and too soon to trusted animal companions. Cataracts took away her sight, and arthritis slowed her gait. She slept more and more. During hot summer days she could be found bathing in the sun's warmth by the door to the patio. Towards the end I would often gently move her; age had dimmed her perception and I worried she would get too warm.

Even as the end approached, and she grew more disoriented, she would still purr incessantly as she sat on my lap, and she was *always* happy to bite me if things annoyed her enough.

Her death that warm spring afternoon left me empty. The end came quickly and without suffering, but it was as if a part of me died with her. There will never be another like her—the old downtown alley cat named Grandma. I gave her another chance and a more comfortable life, but she gave me far more than that. In trying times and in good times she was a true friend. In this life there is no greater gift.

Jasper

KIMBERLEE CURTIS

GLANCING UP AT THE CLOCK, I snapped the notebook shut. Five of ten…the early morning paperwork complete, it was time to face the public. I picked up my keys and ambled across the lobby. Outside, only one man waited, a reprieve from the lines of most days during that long summer.

"Good Morning," I smiled as I unlocked the glass door.

"Hi, uh, I found a dog on I-95," the man mumbled with downcast eyes. "I need something to bring it in with."

My mind immediately started to assess the situation. His body language and lack of eye contact made me wonder about the credibility of his story. I walked back around the corner, selected a blue nylon slip leash from the bundles on the wall and handed it to him.

While he was outside, I picked out a yellow identification tag and began filling out an incoming stray slip.

A few minutes passed, and he returned *carrying* a young adult Doberman. "She won't walk," he said, "but I don't think she's hurt."

When I began asking questions about when and where he had found the dog, his manner shifted from discomfort to brusqueness.

"Look, I was at the toll gate on the highway and I saw it

running around. I didn't want to see it get hit, OK? I'm already late." With that he handed me the leash and left quickly.

I glanced down at the motionless heap of dog. She had open, festering sores on her left hip and several raw patches on her side. I reached towards her carefully...she had the stiff, tense posture that signaled caution should be used.

She didn't move a muscle as I stroked her wide brown head. Her eyes were huge amber orbs, filled with fear. I kept up a constant stream of soothing talk to her, feeling her muscles stiffen as I slipped the collar with an identification tag on it around her neck.

Just about then, one of the kennel attendants came through the door into the lobby, and the two of us tried to coax her to stand. But she wouldn't budge. Laughing at ourselves, we ended up gently sliding her across the tiled lobby floor and into the small exam room where I gave her a distemper vaccination. She didn't even flinch.

We finally managed, between pushing and carrying her, to get her back to the kennels, where she slithered underneath the bench in her run to hide.

Returning to the front desk, I went back to work, but the thought of those great marble eyes nagged at my soul all morning. The poor animal wasn't mean, just paralyzed with fear. As soon as my lunch break came, I headed straight back to her run and found her sitting up.

After talking to her for a while, I gingerly opened the gate and slid halfway in her run with her, crouching down with the door partially between us. I still wanted to be careful around her. I felt her weight shift against me. Slowly, her front paw moved up to rest on my knee. Those owl-like eyes begged me to stay longer, and I did.

After months of scrupulously avoiding emotional involvement with hundreds of dogs and cats, I finally broke. Tears rolled down my cheeks as I stifled a sob. She had reached the place I always guarded.

After her three-day holding period as a stray, and after many daily visits, I began to take her outside. Her leash manners were excellent. So despite the protests of some kennel workers who still mistrusted those colossal eyes and subdued behavior, she was put up for adoption.

Our veterinary technician and the on-call animal control officer began taking her outside after the gates were locked at night. They discovered she had a passion for frisbee-chasing and a playful side.

As the days passed, only a few queries were made about her, and they were all of the I-need-a-guard-dog-to-chain-up variety. People looking for a dog for the wrong reasons are attracted to Dobermans and certain other breeds because they mistakenly think such dogs are "tough" or "mean." Nothing could be further from the truth.

She began coughing on Monday morning, and I knew this might be it—if she was getting sick, she would have to be put down. I persuaded the staff to wait before they pulled her so I could talk to my parents. They had been considering another Dobe. Their female was elderly and suffered frequent hip dysplasia problems; it might be just the right time to add a new member to the family.

I brought her to their farm. My father's protests were quelled the moment she sat next to him and slipped her head under his resting hand.

"So what are we going to call her?"

We decided upon Jasper, a semi-precious stone the red-rust of her sparse coat.

It's now three years later. Jasper and my father are practically inseparable. The two of them were made for one another. My father was never one to fuss over the family dogs as we grew up, but he babies Jasper like a child. Her coat has filled out to a brilliant chocolate brown and the raw patches are healed and long gone. She is the picture of perfect health.

She had obviously been trained well somewhere along the way, and already knew all basic commands when I brought her home to dad. Her passion for frisbees keeps dad exercising on a daily basis, and she delights the entire family.

I think I knew deep-down from the moment she put her paw on my knee in that kennel that she would become a part of our family. I kept telling myself something would work out. There are rare moments in life when you're absolutely sure everything will turn out for the best; happily for Jasper, and for the rest of us, this was one of them.

A Christmas Carol

DIANE ALLEVATO

TINY TIM SAT SILENTLY like a baby buddha in a towel-lined shoebox. He was four weeks old and his unblinking gray-blue eyes matched his gray-blue fur.

Out of the shoebox and into the cupped palm of my hands, a teacup kitten found alone on a front lawn.

Armed with jars of baby food and good intentions, I carried Tim home for four weeks of routine growing up. But Tim wouldn't eat the Gerbers and mealtimes were spitting, gagging, forced feedings. He wouldn't eliminate, even with simulated mother cat assistance and he wouldn't or couldn't walk. Kittens often lack grace but Tim was beyond grace—he was crippled.

A series of X-rays revealed a fragile transparent bone structure. Diagnosis: malnourishment. Treatment: a well-balanced, mineral-rich diet. But how do you convince an unweaned kitten to eat lots of what's good for him? I sought advice. I fretted and worried. I prepared a smorgasbord of puréed foodstuffs. Tim just whimpered at mealtimes and slept in between. Perhaps his fate had been sealed and I was being unkind to rip open the envelope. I set a deadline—Friday morning.

On Friday morning Tim woke up, found and used his litter box, ate a saucer of kitten chow *pâté* and scampered up my leg. We rushed to the shelter to announce Tim's remarkable recovery and display his prowling, pouncing prowess. He would make it.

The sad news is that Tiny Tim is not Typical Tim. The fate of the vast majority of foundlings is decided by those who let cats breed. While the number of unwanted puppies has fallen sharply over the last five years in many areas of the country, kittens continue to arrive at shelters by the baskets, bags and boxes. The most fragile of baby animals, they often succumb to infections, digestive problems, or respiratory diseases. The "miracle" of their birth is more often a tragic tale of suffering and premature death for kittens who are abandoned before they have even been weaned.

But for now the spirit of this year's holiday season is reflected in the gray-blue eyes of this tiny cat who will spend his first Christmas in a new home.

"God bless us, every one." – Tiny Tim.

Desert Duty

JAN ELSTER

AUTHOR'S NOTE: *Herding dogs are bred for a very specific purpose, and when they don't do their job, many ranchers don't keep them around. Milly's fatal flaw was that she would not work sheep. The several ranchers who tried her out were unsuccessful in training Milly to work their flocks, so she was eventually turned into a humane society. She was weary with worms, weighed only twenty-five pounds, and was nursing two pups. Her teeth were stubs, worn down from chewing on the chain to which she had been tethered for much of her life.*

Our connection was immediate and she adopted me. After spending several years in California, we moved to the Sonoran Desert in Arizona. We both belong here. We faithfully walk up and down the dry river bed every day, sharing canine and human perspectives on the sun, sand and saguaros. But they were wrong about Milly. Now nine years old, forty-five pounds, healthy and alert, she has taken to ranch work in her own way. She herds tennis balls, prairie dogs, twigs, baby quail, lizards, paper clips, her own shadow and me. We've come home together.

I ADMIT IT. MY DOG, MILLY, sleeps with me. She politely curls up on the foot of the bed, assuredly leaning against my calf or laying her chin across my ankle. I would not make public notice of this except for how her behavior has shifted over the last few months.

Milly used to stay the night. Now, when it is time to stretch out in bed, read for fifteen minutes and then turn off the lights, Milly leaps up to join me, waits for her nightly ear rub, looks me straight in the eyes to make sure everything is in order, and then retreats to the bedroom's floor-to-ceiling sliding glass window with a view overlooking the desert. Positioning herself in the window like a sphinx, she takes in the desert—all night long. Even though it is pitch black outside, or the moon's rays are casting only a pale light, she maintains her Egyptian bearing. She waits and watches. For what, I'm not sure. But every time I wake up and glance her way, I see the shadowed outline of her oversized ears perked at attention, her front paws crossed, and her eyes fixated on what looks to me like mounds of sand and clumps of cactus.

Milly's demeanor, her absolute silence and her eight hours of undaunted attention out the window all tell me that the desert is alive at night with creatures that captivate her interest and entertain her soul. My imagination says there must be lizards holding community get-togethers, spiders building condominiums, crickets sawing overtime, pack rats gathering the things they love, javelina making havoc of the prickly pear and perhaps even coyotes yawning and stretching so silently that only kindred canine spirits can hear. When I get up for a drink of water in the night, Milly switches to her other job—herding me safely to the bathroom sink. She watches over me intently, making sure I do not stub my toe, walk into a wall, or do anything else out of the ordinary. Then she escorts me back to bed. Her mission successfully accomplished, she returns to desert duty. Sphinx-like again. Watching. Silently patrolling.

It always happens just before daylight begins to creep in the room and terminate the darkness of night. Just minutes before the mourning doves begin to coo, the quail families commence their scurrying up and down sand mounds, the cactus wren launches into her daily scoldings, and the prairie dogs begin their dashing about, Milly leaps onto the bed. She pokes her nose into whichever of my ears is available, scans the situation, and then

curls up on the foot of the bed. She assumes her position, leaning
against my calf or laying her chin across my ankle, and she goes to
sleep. Her nighttime vigil is over. Her desert duty is done. She
ceases being whatever it is she becomes when the desert is dark,
and is once again my faithful companion, who will, within the
hour, rise with me, stretch her legs, get ready for a morning walk
and watch me with that gaze of hers, as if to say, "What's next for
us?"

But Milly has secrets. She has a direct line. She knows what
goes on in the desert when it is dark and the rest of us are sleeping,
replenishing ourselves for the day ahead. How I wish I could
assume the sphinx-like position, see what she sees and know what
she knows. I can only guess about what goes on, but Milly knows
all the history that is being made every night by the desert creatures.

Could Milly's secret be that she only watches the shadowy
desert because it is entertaining? Or is it that every night an
ancient yearning inside her calls? Do her instincts tell her she
really is queen of the nighttime desert? Could she be remembering
a time when she ran with the swiftest of the *canis latrans,* "God's
Dogs," as the Navajo call the coyote, catching jackrabbits in mid-
air or going for weeks without water? I do not know. The secret is
hers, not to be shared with me. I am jealous, and I am in awe.

So yes, it is true, Milly very briefly sleeps with me every night.
But only after she has returned from desert duty.

Titrations

L. DIANNE WASHEK

GREYHOUND FRIENDS *is one of many organizations nationwide that specializes in rescuing, sheltering and placing specific breeds. Greyhounds were revered companions in ancient Egypt and Rome, and during the Middle Ages the elegant and docile animals were symbols of status and privilege. Greyhound racing is only a recent phenomenon. It is currently legal in eighteen states.*

Of the many needs the dogs have when they come to Grey-hound Friends' shelter, medical care ranks high on the list. Like many shelters, Greyhound Friends relies on skilled volunteers to provide foster care for ailing animals. The animals are cared for until they are ready for permanent placement.

I HEARD ABOUT THE TERRIBLE plight of racing grey-hounds when I was in nursing school. I knew that barely fifteen percent of those bred for racing ever even made it to the track (the rest are weaned out of the litter). I was aware that tens of thousands of the dogs that didn't perform up to expectation or were past their racing prime were destroyed annually. I had heard that most of the animals lived out lives of loneliness and discomfort. I knew that unscrupulous breeders, thinking there is money to be made from the sport of greyhound racing, brought even more of these unfortunate creatures into the world. The poor conditions under which so many of these once revered animals lived saddened me deeply, and I vowed that one day I would do whatever I could to help them and prevent the terrible wasting of life.

The time finally came. I had already adopted my own rescued greyhound when I realized I could put my professional skills to work to help other greyhounds. I am a nurse with a special interest in wound healing. I knew one way I could make a difference would be to provide foster care for injured greyhounds who were too sick to remain at Greyhound Friends' shelter. It was in this way that Dianne's Recuperative Center began!

Greyhounds sustain injuries while racing and as a result of fights and other mishaps at racing kennels and farms. Their wounds can get infected and quickly become life-threatening. Under normal conditions a healthy dog eating a well-balanced diet has the ability to fight an infection and rebuild healthy tissue. But racing greyhounds are almost always kept underweight, and often they are too debilitated and depleted of the nutrients they need for a normal healing process to take place. Sometimes the dogs are in relatively good health and a simple suture will do the job. But more often the dogs I see are in very poor shape and do not have "easy" injuries.

I remember my first patient, Johnnie. He was a beautiful black and white spotted male. The director of Greyhound Friends had told me he was in "kind of" bad shape. She asked me if I would take him home for a while. He was laying on a soft blanket in his run as Louise and I approached. He was filthy and tick-infested. He looked up at us in a haze of exhaustion and pain with angelic eyes. He had a bandage around the full circumference of his chest. One of his front legs had most of the skin ripped off. I had no way of knowing the extent of his chest wound, but it was obvious that his leg wound was very severe. All of the exposed flesh was filthy and it was doubtful if his skin borders could be sewn together. As we walked towards him, he looked up and managed a little wag of his tail. That was as much energy as he could muster. We gently helped him to his feet and ever so slowly and carefully we walked him to my car so I could take him to the veterinarian. Not a complaint or whimper came out of this courageous boy! My heart broke for all the others, who, injured or not, had not made it to a safe haven like Johnnie had.

Johnnie was in surgery for several hours. His chest wound was several inches long and cut deep enough to expose his chest bone. Sewing the wound edges together was almost impossible, and several times his sutures tore. Weeks turned into months, and eventually we were forced to just let the leg tissue and chest wound granulate by themselves. Johnnie finally recovered and now lives a happy life with a family in Boston, Massachusetts.

Jesse had a five-inch opening along his groin and thigh. Worse even than that though was his neck wound. This was a gash from below his chin to the bottom of his neck. For added measure, a two to three inch wound crossed the gash diagonally. Jesse was a beautiful jet black dog who didn't know the meaning of the word "slow." He energetically ignored his serious injuries. He made many trips to the doctor, but finally metal stitches did the trick.

Wardell was a wonderful gray brindled greyhound with a badly infected leg. He had a temperature of 106 degrees, was lethargic and had a racing heart. His leg had swollen to twice its normal size. We placed ice packs all over his body to bring down his temperature. After surgery I took him home to convalesce, placing him on pillows with his leg elevated above his heart to decrease the swelling and pain. He slept for two days and woke only for feedings and to eliminate. Not a peep came out of him during wound care and dressing changes. I was afraid he wouldn't be able to grow back enough tissue to cover and refill his wound, which went all the way down to exposed tendon. Eventually this handsome boy healed beautifully and went off to a new life.

People ask, "Doesn't it depress you that you work so hard and yet only a few are rescued?" To this I answer that when I studied chemistry, we had a container of liquid that was of one color and substance. To change its color and properties we added one drop at a time of another color until finally the last drop changed the whole property and color of that liquid. This is called titrating. I deeply believe that each drop of goodness collects somewhere and one day these drops will all add up to make one big wonderful change. This is what we are all doing. Until the rest of the world discovers how important and necessary it is to care for animals, we must keep titrating—until the whole thing changes to the color we want.

The Real Cinderella

PAUL GLASSNER

THE SAN FRANCISCO SPCA has a special fund that is named for a fairy tale. As in the fictional tale, the Cinderella Fund helps those who have lived in misery find happy endings. And so it happened for a dog named Mandy, who, like Cinderella, lived life in cinders as an outcast.

Mandy was found wandering the streets, an abandoned animal. From the way she was walking when she was found, it appeared she was either sick or injured. The humane officer who found her on the city street took her straight to the shelter's hospital. But the veterinarian on duty had great difficulty examining his patient. He could barely see her.

From head to toe and nose to tail the little dog was covered with a mass of filthy, dirty, tangled fur. She stood less than a foot high, yet two-foot-long mats were dragging behind her like so many heavy chains. Twisted, lumpy braids hung from her face. Wherever she stepped on the examination table, dust fell from her like soot from a chimney. Offered a dish of water, she bent her head down and clumps of hair dangling from her face fell in, turning the water muddy brown as she drank.

Carol Cooper, the shelter's grooming instructor, was called in. After looking Mandy over, she said she had never seen a dog in worse condition. She estimated the dog must have been wandering the streets for at least a year. Mandy's severely matted coat had been neglected so long that in many places it was knotted up like rope and was pulling at her skin. It meant that with every step Mandy was suffering pain. Down the length of her back was a single flat chunk of congealed fur and filth that was as hard and thick as a stoneware plate.

Carol and a few skilled assistants clustered around Mandy with the deliberateness of surgeons. They went to work right away. Slowly, gently, meticulously, they cut and clipped, often hair by hair, down through the layers, always being cautious not to pinch or pull. In a particularly delicate procedure, the groomers carefully snipped away at the base of the large mat on Mandy's back, peeling it upwards ever so slowly, snipping and lifting until at last it fell on the floor with a thud.

The process was surely a traumatic one for the street urchin, yet this little dog, who had probably never in her life been brushed or groomed, and who was probably now enduring considerable pain, was at every opportunity licking the hands and faces of the people attending to her. Getting attention perhaps for the first time since puppyhood, the little dog seemed to sense that she was at last in caring hands. With skilled strokes of the scissors and clippers, Mandy's attendants stripped the entanglements from her body.

Her overall condition, including the smell she exuded, was horrible enough, but the groomers were even more astonished when they got to her legs. Here the mats were like casts up to Mandy's shoulders—no wonder she had a hard time walking! After these encumbrances were painstakingly peeled off, Mandy was still not moving normally. The groomers could feel how weak her muscles were. Evidently, her movements had been impaired for so long that the muscles had atrophied from disuse.

Mandy's attendants moved her from the table to the tub, where they removed filthy clots of material from her ears, gave her a much-needed flea bath, and shampooed away the last traces of her life on the streets. After two-and-one-half hours, they finally knew what they were dealing with: Mandy was a black (not brown or gray) sweet-faced Maltese mix. After a pedicure to trim overgrown toenails and a blow-dry, Mandy was ready to meet a prince.

Back in the hospital, she was discovered to be in remarkable shape despite her ordeal. Mandy was an adult dog, but she had the diminutive size and attitude of a puppy. However, her rib cage was easily visible and her legs were quite stiff. She was weak and needed lots of rest and nutritional recuperation. Still, her most noticeable feature was the way she kept licking all the hands that came near her!

It was on the second day of her convalescence that she met the man who would be her prince. On a tour of the shelter that day was a young, animal-loving couple. The first stop on their tour was the hospital. After everyone had shuffled in, the guide began describing the medical facilities to the group. Richard and Darla didn't hear a word; they were busy meeting Mandy.

After the tour they asked to stop by her quarters again. Two days later Richard came back to check on her. "She came over to lick my hand right away," he recalls. "She was so friendly after everything she had been through. We wanted that dog to find a very good home."

A few days passed. Mandy grew stronger and was moved to the adoption ward. Volunteers gave the little dog short walks to begin getting her muscles back in tone. Mandy was selected to appear in media ads as an adoptable Pet-of-the-Week. A few more days went by.

Then Richard called again to check on Mandy and see if she had been adopted. She hadn't. "We weren't looking for another dog," remembers Richard, "but I couldn't stop thinking about her." That afternoon he came in and adopted her.

The prince could not be more pleased. "She is the sweetest girl," he says. "The minute she's awake, that tail is going. She follows me all over the house. She's learned to play ball and she and our Welsh terrier play tag. Mandy is very curious and not afraid of anything. Her coat is growing back beautifully—she has soft, black fur. Everyone who meets her wants to take her home."

"I think Mandy was somebody's pet once upon a time. She so appreciates getting love. She knows people, she knows what it is to get affection, and I think she's making up for a lot of lost time. She's also used to sleeping in a bed," he says with a laugh. "And," he adds quickly, "she hasn't stopped eating since she got here."

A neglected soul. A life among the cinders. A guardian angel. An almost magical transformation. A fateful encounter. And a new life lived happily ever after. Is this the story of Cinderella—or of Mandy?

Fairy tales aren't the only stories with happy endings.

Hello, Dolly

DIANE ALLEVATO

I UNLOCKED THE DOOR to the stray dog kennels and began my morning rounds of visiting our shelter guests. I don't remember opening the first door on the left. Somehow it just swung open and a brown and white and black baby dog leaped the enclosure into my arms.

I was not looking for a dog. I was doing my job. I was certainly not looking for a puppy. I just wanted to see if she was as soft as she looked. I took her home for a few days to help socialize her. I bought her a green nylon collar because the shelter identification band was too institutional. I bought a few rawhide chews and some squeaky toys just to keep her from underfoot. I bought a bag of premium puppy food just so she would get off to a good start. I had a friend shoot two rolls of film of her for purely artistic reasons. I borrowed a crate for my office, just to keep things businesslike. I brought in an old crate from the garage to my bedroom because if you are keeping a puppy for a few days, you might as well start housebreaking her.

And then I called a few friends and asked if I was too old for a puppy. I was losing my objectivity.

I went for a walk with my dog Sarah. I asked her about the puppy. I anthropomorphize enough to ask the question, but not enough to expect a spoken answer. Her eyes seemed to say, "I will be thirteen in the spring, too young for an early retirement. I can break a new dog into the routine: Teach her manners, how to patrol shelter luncheons and potlucks without being banished to the office; how to distinguish between our own cat and others; how to put off strangers and welcome friends..."

We went for a walking interview with a Samoyed friend. I took her to tea with my sister's cats. I watched the faces of co-workers. I tried to divine the thoughts of volunteers and visitors.

What normal healthy person would adopt a puppy, I pondered, if they considered: Fifteen years of maintenance and veterinary care, six to eight hours a week out-of-doors even in January, more fleas, revised travel plans, the scourge of foxtails and ticks, an aging cranky cat, a beloved older dog. There were so many compelling reason why not and one compelling reason why. Sometime in those five days of interviews, introductions, ruminations, and conversations, I grew to love her.

She tumbles, ten-weeks-old, across the grass, with a rubber squeaky tennis shoe in her mouth. "Well, hello Dolly!" I laugh as she hurls herself into my face.

Impound #S132202

REBECCA D. WINTER

I WAS CLEANING UP as part of my volunteer duties at the municipal animal shelter that Saturday morning when I heard an odd sound coming from one of the lower cages. I bent forward and peered into the back corner. A small black cat with medium-length fur and enormous, terrified green eyes was staring at me. The thin creature was sitting with its bony chest tight against the back of the cage, its head tilted backwards at a forty-five degree angle, surveying me.

I stood up and read the information card attached to the cage door. "Impound #S132202. Black. Female. Adult. Thin. PG. Left in box, front of shelter." It was dated that morning. The "PG" notation made my heart sink. In practical terms, a pregnant cat is almost certainly doomed. If an owner has not claimed it during its holding period (which isn't likely), the cat and her kittens—if they have been born—are usually euthanized.

I leaned back down and looked at the creature. "Hi, there," I said softly. Her eyes got a bit bigger, but there was no grumble. "Will you let me hold you?" I carefully reached in the cage and held my left hand toward her to sniff.

She was so frightened she didn't even smell my fingers. I reached in with my right hand and grasped the nape of her neck, while pulling her out of the cage with my left hand cradling her underneath her front legs. I could feel the fullness of the kittens she was carrying. She looked up at me and made eye contact; something stirred behind those eyes and spoke to me. "Yes, yes, it's okay now," I murmured softly.

I snuggled her close and she clung with all four feet to my chest, like a stuffed toy outfitted with Velcro strips. She buried her face in my neck and began to shiver, her ribs tiny beneath my fingers; I felt my heart go out to this little cat, and I knew I had to save her. "Don't be afraid, sweet pea," I cooed to her.

Since I was a registered volunteer foster parent, I decided to apply to foster this special little cat. She would be spayed (which would abort the kittens), and then I could care for her at home, spending as long as necessary to socialize her so she could be put up for adoption and placed in a permanent home. I filled out the paperwork, put a note on her impound card, helped the veterinary technician with her examination (she was found to be malnourished and grossly underweight, but otherwise remarkably healthy), and took her over to the shelter hospital ward. "Don't worry little one; you only have to stay here a few days, then you'll be home with me," I assured her. I checked the spay/neuter surgery calendar and found I would be able to take her home the following Thursday.

I finished my duties elsewhere in the shelter and returned to the hospital to say goodbye. The dim light and soft music had soothed her somewhat. Though her eyes were still huge, she didn't seem alarmed when I slowly reached in to pet her. "You're a beautiful girl, aren't you," I said in a reassuring tone.

Sunday morning I reported for duty and went directly to the hospital to say hello. She definitely recognized me, and leaned forward and sniffed my hand when I reached in to pet her, and she didn't quake when I held her. I was thrilled at the progress! "Just a few more days and you'll be home," I whispered to her as I gently laid her back in the hospital cage.

Monday I went to check on her at 5:00 P.M. As soon as I

walked into the hospital, I could hear the same low grumble I had heard the day I first met her.

I went to her cage and looked in. Something was terribly wrong with her back leg. I was sure this explained why she was growling. Talking softly, I opened the cage and reached in to pet her and examine her leg more closely. The growling stopped and she rubbed her head against my hand. I was ecstatic at the display of trust! With my left hand I gingerly felt her limb. Rather than finding a cat leg in my hand, I found a kitten!

As a responsible pet owner I would never allow my own animals to reproduce, but a part of me couldn't help being pleased at the prospect of fostering a batch of adorable kittens. When I returned Tuesday night, there was a total of three kittens. My friend was busy cleaning her little wriggling babies when I approached her cage. She laid her ears flat on her head and growled. "It's me, mom cat!" I said as I opened the cage door. She stood and rubbed against my hand, three tiny bodies rolling off her side. One was white, one black, and the third a combination of the two colors. Despite their diminutive size, each made quite a bit of racket. They were already exhibiting clear signs of individuality in their activity levels, the tone of their meows, and the way they reacted to being held aloft alongside their mother. After mama cat laid back down, I lined up the babies; they scooted and crawled around to their preferred nipples and set about the task of growing into fat, healthy kittens.

I went to the shelter office to talk to Debra, the volunteer supervisor and the woman who would decide on my foster application, to let her know I could take the kittens too. She had left for the day, so I wrote a note asking her to call me and let me know if I could pick all of them up on Thursday.

When I returned to say goodnight to my friend, her ears stayed folded back and her low grumbling did not stop when I put my hand in the cage, even with my reassuring whispers. She let me pet her though, and I wrote her recalcitrance off to stress and being overwhelmed by all the events of the last few days.

Wednesday night I prepared the house. I set up a bed, eating area, and a litter pan for my new family. I went to sleep thinking about the foursome that would be joining me, and awoke Thursday morning excited.

About 10:00 A.M., Debra called. "Hi, Rebecca. How are you?"

"Fine! How's my family doing?" I asked.

There was a pause on the other end of the phone. It was long enough that I knew something was wrong. "Well," Debra started. Her voice sounded a bit unsteady. When she took a deep breath I knew something was wrong.

"What is it, Debra?" I asked cautiously.

"I've thought a great deal about this and talked to the rest of the staff, Rebecca, and I'm afraid the cat you want to foster is just not adoptable. I am so sorry."

My heart was sinking. "But why ?" I asked.

"She nearly bit an animal care technician, and growls whenever anyone tries to touch her. I hope you understand."

No, I thought to myself, I don't understand. My initial reaction of anger was tempered a bit though when I reminded myself of Debra's professionalism and her devotion to the welfare of animals. I also had the practical realization that she was my supervisor and had absolute authority over these kinds of decisions.

I swallowed and got the words out, "Well, I had my heart set on this cat; maybe she's just upset from giving birth and will settle down."

"I had hoped that too, but I've seen many cats like her. She's been stressed to the point of no return. Our experience is that when a cat acts like this someone is seriously injured or the adoption is a failure."

I thought quickly and decided to wait until I could see Debra in person to press the little cat's case. "I respect your decision, Debra, but I'd like to come and see her and talk to you about it in person, if that's okay."

"Of course," Debra responded. "I know you must be very disappointed. We do have an exceptionally sweet and very loving neutered male orange tabby named Sunny that I wanted to talk to you about. We need a foster home for him. The adoption kennel is overflowing with cats. If I can't make arrangements for him, I'm afraid he'll have to be euthanized. He's already tentatively on the schedule for this morning. Do you think you might be interested? If so, I could hold him for you so you could meet him and see what you think."

"Sure, I'll come by on my lunch hour and we can talk about it," I said as I glanced at the clock.

"I'll see you in a couple of hours then."

We exchanged goodbyes and hung up.

I excused myself and went down the hall to the women's room where I stayed until I my tears stopped. When lunchtime came, I drove to the shelter to meet my big orange tom and say goodbye to the tiny black cat and her little family.

When I walked in to the hospital ward and looked in her cage, my friend was hunkered in the far corner, her kittens gathered behind her. She snarled, teeth bared, lips curled, and slapped at me with her paw, claws extended. "Sweetie, sweetie," was all I could say. Her pupils were slits, even in the dim light, and her muscles were poised for flight and attack should the cage door open. She was operating on pure instinct; thousands of years of domestication were all for naught. She was feeling none of the trust I thought we had established over the last few days.

I had still been hoping that Debra was wrong, that her interpretation of this cat's behavior could be changed through my calm and sensible explanations and arguments. Seeing this coiled black ball of fury though, I realized Debra was right and I resigned myself to accepting her judgement. Someone, somewhere along the way had shirked their responsibility to this cat by not spaying and then abandoning her. She now knew no other way to live than by her raw feline instincts. My friend's fate was sealed.

I had come to terms with the fact I could not save every cat that crossed my path. Even if I had succeeded in saving this one, there would be another one that wouldn't make it. I knew intellectually that when a choice had to be made between saving feral or semi-feral cats and friendly cats with strong pet potential, the wild cats lost. "Goodbye, little black cat. I'm sorry."

With tears in my eyes and stones in my heart, I walked around the corner to meet my orange tom. The cattery was overflowing with lovely cats. Forty almond eyes watched me enter—but no orange tom that I could see anywhere. I shut my eyes and felt a dread; I couldn't take it if he had been put down. I couldn't bear to lose two in one day.

I rushed to the front counter and asked for Debra to be paged. She came out and greeted me. "Hi! You won't believe what happened! At 11:30 A.M., thirty minutes after he had been scheduled for euthanasia, a family came in and adopted Sunny. I hope you realize your willingness to foster him saved his life." She headed down the hall and motioned for me to follow.

"I have something to show you. Look." She pointed at an upper cage where a young cat was waiting for her health examination. I looked in and saw golden eyes in a tiny, fuzzy black face. A wee voice let out a squeak of a meow.

"Hi, darlin'," I crooned to her as I opened the cage door. The small creature flopped over on her back, and put all four feet in the air, even though she was thick with kittens and awkward. The instant I touched her, the room rumbled with a happy purr.

"Debra, could I...," I began.

Yes, of course. That's why I wanted you to meet her. I'll go fill out the paperwork while you take her in for her exam. I've already had the veterinary technician look her over—she's healthy, just a little thin and malnourished. We'll set things up so you can take her home."

"Thanks, Debra," was all I could say as I gathered my new little friend in my arms and held her close.

Epitaph for a Friendship

LAURA A. MORETTI

THE MOUSER-CAT DIED TODAY.
It had been thirteen years since Dad had agreed to allow the shelter-adopted cat to share my life, so long as she would live in the barn to off the mice who came in to steal the horse's grain. But when I brought the tiny black-and-white kitten home that day and showed her to him, he said, "You can't put that little thing out in the barn. She'll freeze to death." So I compromised. The kitten lived in my bedroom and we called her Mouser (or, more affectionately, "The Mouser-Cat"—to keep Dad happy).

And Mouser, I think, wanted to live up to her end of the agreement as well. She pretended to be the most aggressive mousing cat ever known to humankind. Except...well...except she didn't seem to know a mouse from a dog. And it was dogs—in all sizes and shapes—that she viciously chased from the house (even the ones who lived in it)! and it was dogs she lay in ambush for in the front yard and chased down the street with me running after her, screaming for their lives.

"You've got to do something about that cat," Mom would warn me. "She's terrorizing the neighborhood."

But I didn't do anything about that cat, and not because I wouldn't, but because I couldn't. Mouser made it clear from the beginning that it was me who belonged to her. She was, it was true, terribly possessive of me. Perhaps, in her own catlike wisdom, she understood my fears of the big wide world and she would live her life protecting me. Raise your voice at me and she would raise hers at you. And Mouser wasn't polite when she got mad, nor was she merely threatening. She was very serious about protecting what belonged to her—and if her voice couldn't convince you of her intent, her claws could.

When my car was stolen, along with my house keys, a lock-smith, hired by the apartment manager, was called to change the door locks. I got an urgent call at work. "You're going to have to come down here after all, ma'am," he said kindly. "Your cat won't let me in the apartment."

But as determined as she was at voicing her opinion, she was equally affectionate—with me, that is; her possession. I would lie on the sofa, tap the center of my chest, and say, "Kiss? Kiss?" and she would oblige me, leap onto my chest, press her forehead against my lips and take as many kisses as a cat could stand. "The things some animals have to endure," she seemed to dryly express on her face, "just to get fed."

She was also an extremely intelligent cat. Traditional cat games were out of the question. Chase a ball? Not on your life (besides, that was something those smelly cowardly *dogs* did). Play with a string? Hardly. No, if you wanted to play with Mouser, you had to play games by rules you learned as you went along. "You throw the ping-pong ball to me," she would say in a way only Mouser could, "and I'll lie here comfortably and hit it back to you. I'm not moving, so if I miss it, *you* fetch it"—as if it was *me* who had wanted to play to begin with and she was merely obliging me.

Mouser preferred, you see, to spend her waking hours eating. And then, of course, she would have to rest before taking a bath or even a nap, and then it was back to the kitchen again. But Mouser seldom failed to remind me that meals were to be served every morning and every night, and when she did fail to remind me, I'd sneak off to work or off to sleep, hoping she would never remember—because Mouser could stand to lose a few pounds.

One night, after forgetting a meal, I had been in bed for a good half-hour when I heard a horrible cat cry at bedside that awoke me. I snapped on the night lamp and leaned over the mattress. Mouser was sitting there, blinking up at me with that, "You thought I'd forget again, didn't you?" expression while a can of Fancy Feast—which apparently she had carried in from the kitchen—sat nestled on the carpet between her front paws.

I laugh about that to this day—but in the split second of that memory, I hear again the eternal silence on the phone line, the vet's voice in my ear, patient, waiting, hollow—like the way my heart felt then: "Do you think we should let her go?" And I could see Mouser, in my mind's eye, lying there on that exam table with memories that had spanned thirteen years. The vet was telling me what I had feared most: Mouser would be dead within the week. Both kidneys and her liver had been consumed by cancer.

And I had the power, at that very moment, and would never have it again, to bring her out of anesthesia, to give us one more week, or one more day, or even one more moment, to say goodbye again.

If she left me, my heart would break; I couldn't bear the pain that hinted at its inevitability: my life would never be the same without her; she had been my best friend since I was a young girl. But I realized, in those long-drawn out minutes on the phone, in my hesitation, that it was *my* life I was fighting for, not hers—and would she ever forgive me for that?

I remembered suddenly the night before Mouser died. We were lying together on the cool kitchen floor. There was a dying light in her gaze that was fixed on the wall beyond me. I don't think I'd realized, even after her lengthy illness, just how sick she was until that night. She had lost so much weight she was merely a skeleton, and she hadn't eaten in days. I couldn't force one more pill down her throat; I wept with guilt when she fought me—as if she *wanted* to die and I wouldn't let her.

And I was weeping that night, the night before she died, lying on the floor with her, asking her with a grief-filled anguish in the hope she would understand my question:

What should I do, Mouser? What do you want me to do in the morning when you go on the table for exploratory surgery; when I may be told your condition is terminal? Do you want me to let you go?

I cried because only Mouser knew what Mouser wanted and we were separated by ineffective special communication.

Or were we?

As we lay there and I asked these questions silently, only my crying audible, a flash of light came into Mouser's dying eyes. She turned her head in my direction and met my gaze. For a long minute that I had wished would be an eternity, she looked at me, almost through me; my eyes filled with tears and hers with an inexplicable smile.

What? I begged her silently. Do you have the answer?

She was only a few inches from my face; she pressed her forehead to my lips and asked me for a kiss.

"Do what is best for me," I believe she said. "I can accept life better than you can; after all these long, full years, I can accept death as well. In the end, doing what's best for me will bring peace to both our lives."

So I did that next day what I believed Mouser had asked for in her kiss.

The kiss goodbye.

"Yes," I finally answered the doctor. "Let her go."

If Mouser's death has taught me anything, I think it would have to be this: it is not an intangible number that we are removing from our midst when we kill the millions of dogs and cats every year in animal shelters across the country. It isn't a single ID number or a solitary statistic that dies when the light in a single dog's or cat's eyes dies. When we kill a million dogs and cats, we're killing a million lives who could touch us and heal us and bring us a kind of joy and warmth and peace in ways our fellow humans cannot. We're robbing a million beings of a million rays of sunlight, a million memories, a million heartbeats, a million lights of life.

We're killing a million Mousers.

That shelter kitten is waiting for you. Go.

Life has more to offer than death.

PART III

KEEPING COMMITMENTS

I expect to pass through this world but once;
Any good thing I can do, or any kindness I can
show to any fellow creature, let me not defer or
neglect it, for I shall not pass this way again.

STEPHEN GRELLET (1773-1855)

One Dog at a Time

DIANA M. BARRETT

19 JULY 1991

I held it in my hand and gazed at it. I'd worked three years to get it and it had finally come. Though I knew I'd do my best, I wondered if I could ever be worthy of it. I wondered who had worn it before me, and if they had pondered it like this when they received it. Mostly though, I wondered who could ever give up Badge #115 and the perfect job that went with it: Animal Control Officer.

20 JULY 1991

I followed my co-worker the length of the building to the Euthanasia Room. While walking past the kennels of dogs, my eyes met countless pairs of brown eyes looking at me. I wondered how my co-worker walked straight ahead, never looking into the cages. He was talking about a movie he had seen the night before. His voice faded gradually as we were separated. I had stopped walking, drawn to one particular run and its occupant. Cage #31, a two-year-old female black Labrador. Her head was held down, her eyes positioned so she looked up at me. Her body posture was submissive and as I spoke to her she began to shiver.

Reality jolted me back. My co-worker was nudging me. "Are you coming?" he asked. "Yeah, yeah, sorry," I mumbled and followed.

That day, my second day on the job, I helped euthanize twenty-

two animals—eighteen dogs and six cats. I had been involved in
putting animals down before when I worked in veterinary hospi-
tals, but this was different. These were *all* healthy, relatively
young, adoptable animals. I knew I'd be putting unwanted animals
to sleep, but I had no idea it would be this many.

26 July 1991
During the next week I became very attached to my friend in
Cage #31. I took her out in the backyard of the shelter almost
every day. We played with a tennis ball a few times, but, mostly we
would just sit together. She had become quite comfortable with
me and would jump around anxiously whenever she saw me
working throughout the day. During that week I tried to find
someone to adopt her, but to no avail. People respond to Black
Labradors as if they are "a dime a dozen," I was told by the more
experienced officers. I even thought about taking her home with
me to my one-room apartment that didn't allow pets. I sadly
realized though that if this were my solution I'd soon have an
apartment full of dogs. I came to the conclusion that I would have
to learn to care for my dog friends and then let go. Cage #31's
occupant was an instrumental friend. On her last day I spent time
playing with her, and telling her what a good dog she was. I
hugged her, and then I ended her life.

During the next six weeks of my training period, I carried out
my work, but I was in and out of emotional shock. I did my best to
hide it though. I was the only woman on staff (except for a supervisor), and I didn't want my male co-workers to think I couldn't
handle the job. I knew there had to be a way to do the job without
closing down emotionally. I just wasn't sure what it was. I wondered how the other officers had found a place inside themselves
to do this job as long as some of them had. I would have to find my
own way, just as they had theirs. For a while my method was to
end my work day by driving two blocks, turning the corner, and

parking, so I could have a good cry. I couldn't believe society could be so irresponsible with animals, that the city would have to hire someone like me to clean up the mess.

9 AUGUST 1991
I had completed my training at the shelter and was now being sent to Las Vegas, Nevada to attend the Animal Control Academy as part of my final certification as a humane officer. It was fascinating to meet people from all over the United States who had the same kinds of goals for their work as I did: to provide a necessary service in the most humane and effective way possible. Toward the end of the course, we attended a day-long workshop on euthanasia. During one portion of the workshop, we broke into small groups to discuss our feelings about the subject. I was intimidated by some of the other officers who already had extensive experience—and I was afraid to say something stupid. So I decided to just listen. Maybe I would learn something. We were given a sheet of questions, and told to discuss them with a partner. I went over the worksheet with a man who had been quiet through most of the session. As we started asking each other questions, what he said shattered me. He was having a recurring dream that he had died and that he was at heaven's gate. All the animals he had put to sleep were there at the gate and wouldn't let him in. How had this man managed to euthanize animals for thirteen years and cope with guilt so intense that he could not escape it even in his dreams? Even more importantly to me, how could I avoid the same kind of fate?

I took a long walk through the streets of Las Vegas that night. It had been a warm day—100 degrees—but with the sun down the temperature had dropped to a cool seventy-eight. That is when it came to me. I remembered my friend in Cage #31 from five weeks before, and the other friends I'd said hello and goodbye to since then. The ones who had not been redeemed by their owners and the ones who were not fortunate enough to be adopted seemed to appreciate the extra attention I gave them. And in a strange way it seemed that because of my effort, *they* made their euthanasias easier on *me*. I had been present emotionally with them through their shelter experience; maybe that connection would be the thing that would make the difference for my friends and I. Only time would tell.

MARCH 1994

Almost three years have passed, and I am still holding to the same philosophy. Each morning when I'm walking the length of the building to go to my truck, I greet the animals, talk to them, encourage them to keep their noses up, or, when time allows, I play just a little with some of them. Four days a week I'm on the road, responsible for the various duties of an animal control officer. Once a week though, I'm in the shelter, helping kennel staff with cleaning and maintenance, and working with the animals. This is the most physically and emotionally demanding day of my week, but I love working directly with the animals in the shelter. I feel great when one of my friends gets reunited with his or her family, or when a stray gets a new family. Sometimes as I'm working during my day in the shelter, a citizen will ask, "You seem to like animals…how do you do this job?" My answer: *One dog at a time.*

How Kato Was Rescued From the Superstition Mountains

GRAHAM PHALEN

THE FIVE OF US worked to fit the horse's legs through the holes of the cargo net while trying to maintain our footing on the treacherously muddy ledge. Kato, the horse, tossed his head and nervously nipped at Duane, who struggled to keep him still.

The horse could sense our urgency. Though we worked quietly and smoothly, placing his tired, shaking legs through the net, we had to be communicating our concern to the exhausted animal. The clouds were closing in rapidly, obscuring the buttes around us. We had only a few minutes to accomplish our task; Kato's ordeal had lasted seven days, and in trying to bring it to a close, we had to do everything right the first time. We might not get a second chance.

It began the previous Sunday, when John Hoffman and two friends rode their horses into the Superstition Mountain Wilderness Area, located roughly fifty miles east of Phoenix, Arizona. They took a wrong turn on the rugged trail. The terrain would have been difficult at best for a skilled hiker; it was extremely taxing for the horses. They came to a bald rock face with a narrow defile cutting down the steep slope. It appeared tricky but passable from where they stood.

It wasn't that easy though. Fifty feet below the trail, they were unable to lead their horses any farther. The rock became smooth and slippery, and below stretched an impassable, barren sandstone grade.

The riders were able to drive two of the horses back up to the trail, but John Hoffman's 1200-pound sorrel gelding, Kato, couldn't make it.

Hoffman and his friends stayed on the mountain two days and two nights, repeatedly trying to urge the horse up the narrow crevice, but Kato's spirit flagged. He only ended up abraded and defeated by the climb.

On Wednesday, Hoffman called me to request the help of the Arizona Humane Society. I organized a small group of volunteers, and we hiked an adjoining trail, Route 233, with him that afternoon. The climb was tough, with thirty- to forty-pound packs of food and water on our backs, but it was worth every step when we saw Kato eagerly eat his rations.

Thursday was much the same. We packed supplies up the two-mile trail that morning, and spent the day improving the steep grade and poor footing the horse would have to climb. Kato ate and rested on a small shelf below the slide. Although he had sustained minor leg injuries, his attitude had improved by late that afternoon.

Friday, a group of fifteen volunteers, including five volunteers from the Central Arizona Mountain Rescue Association, attempted to assist Kato up the cleft using a system of pulleys and an improvised harness. With five of us working with the horse and the rest on the ropes, we managed to get Kato twenty feet up the base of the climb, but could not urge him further. Despite long periods of rest and a slow pace, the combination of stress and exhaustion took its toll. He would approach the climb, leaning for support on the harness, only to collapse on his side with a groan. Leg wraps kept him from injuring himself seriously, but we decided not to risk overstressing him. While our veterinarian, Dr. Carol Spillers, examined Kato, Jerry Foster from local television station KPNX helicoptered in on SKY 12 and dropped us some supplies. He felt we could have the horse airlifted out. We agreed to try the lift Saturday morning, and left Kato eating his ration of alfalfa pellets.

Saturday was a discouraging day. The Superstitions were completely socked in with heavy fog and rain. Foster, flying SKY 12, and pilot Gary Mercer, flying a helicopter donated by Air Services International, were unable to fly with the low ceiling, but stayed on standby in case of a break in the weather.

A small group of us once more ascended the trail, equipped with food and water. The trek was made doubly difficult with constant rain, dense fog, slippery rock, and soggy clothing. I reasoned that if I was uncomfortable, Kato had to be miserable.

When we reached Kato's ledge, we found him soaked and shivering, standing on what was now a slippery incline of mud and water. We rubbed him down and made a makeshift blanket out of Foster's cargo net and sheets and ponchos of plastic. We waited for a break in the weather while Kato warmed up and ate, but realized that, with ice particles floating through the fog and a ten-mile-per-hour wind, hypothermia was a real possibility for our team. I left Kato to stay one more night on the soggy little ledge, wrapped as warmly as we could make him.

Sunday arrived with much the same weather. Low clouds and rain swirled intermittently around the sandstone knob where Kato was trapped. Dr. Spillers felt that Kato couldn't take much more exposure. We had to get him out that day; another storm was reported on its way. We called in our two volunteer pilots, while fourteen members of the Apache Junction Helicopter Rescue Team stood by to assist in the lift attempt. At around 10:15 A.M., the clouds began to break around the summit.

We scrambled to take advantage of the break and quickly assembled the rescue team. Jerry Foster airlifted Dr. Spillers to the landing zone, followed by Arizona Humane Society Lieutenant Duane Adams and myself. We were to handle the horse. Apache

Junction Mountain Rescue's Gene Berry and Art Tice were flown up to assist us.

Kato was fairly dry, but tired and shaking from standing on the muddy ledge. He had become entangled in his muddy blanket, and we had a few anxious moments unwrapping him while he struggled to maintain his balance.

We faced the most difficult part of our task. While maneuvering on the narrow, slippery perch, we were to position the horse in the net so that he would be properly balanced for the airship, unable to fall forward or backward during the flight, and be able to breathe properly. If he slipped or went down in the mud while we positioned the net, we were sunk. If he spooked or fussed, he could send us flying off the narrow shelf or seriously injure us. The pilot would lift the horse slightly to test the load, but we would probably only have one real chance. The weather was worsening.

We positioned the center of the net under Kato's girth, in line with his withers. We then placed his front legs through the holes in the net, careful not to risk splaying his legs or cutting off his wind at the neck. Duane, at the horse's head, quieted him as we placed his rear legs through. We were forced to cut the webbing to get the net over his hocks. He fidgeted and fought to get his footing on the slick incline. We had to be careful not to compromise the integrity of the net. After ten minutes of careful work, we were finished.

Next was a crucial step in the mission. Dr. Spillers was flown back to base camp, where John Hoffman, Kato's owner, and several volunteers waited to receive the horse. Gary Mercer, piloting Air Services International's Bell Long Ranger helicopter, lifted off and ascended with Jerry Foster in SKY 12 alongside, to relay radio instructions.

On the ledge, the four of us watched the choppers approach. Gene guided them by radio, while Art, Duane and I positioned the net and steadied the horse. After the initial gust from the rotor wash, Mercer expertly placed the end of the 100-foot cargo cable on the nearby rock to ground out its charge. After the flight up, the cable had collected enough static electricity to knock a man off his feet.

Despite all the strange noise and activity, Kato remained fairly quiet. We passed the hook through the four corner rings, while Mercer held his ship and the cable rock-steady. The slack was gently taken up until the net was almost taut.

Gene gave the thumbs up signal, and Mercer gently lifted Kato upwards. He was startled, but after a few minor crow hops, he was lifted a couple of feet off the ground to hang placidly.

We all looked at each other and instantly agreed: we had to do it, now. The thick clouds were rolling in fast; there wouldn't be another chance. With cries of, "Go! Go! Go!," we signaled the pilot up, and Kato was on his way. The horse remained calm and quiet in the net, looking around curiously as he was gradually carried down the valley in a low level flight.

As I climbed along the rock face to watch their descent, I experienced a great surge of elation and relief. We weren't out of the woods yet, but at least the exhausted animal was on his way down.

Then came the voice over the radio: "Kato is down and OK!" We all cheered, shaking hands and grinning ear to ear, ecstatic at the good news. I don't think I've ever felt so good.

After the flight from the mountain back to meet our exhilarated group on the ground, I looked up the valley and saw clouds once again obscuring the knob. I reflected on our good fortune. A potentially dangerous and risky operation had ended in triumph. Our friend was back on level ground, contentedly munching hay, his happy owner smiling quietly by his side. With the hard work, commitment and cooperation of some dedicated volunteers, and the care and skill of two fine helicopter pilots, we had done it. Kato was safe.

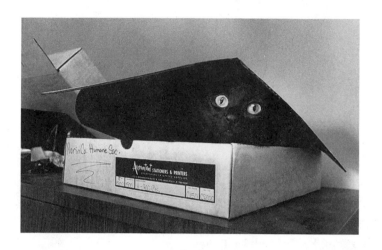

For Gray Cat

AMY SHAPIRO

SUNDAY

A friend and I take our dogs for a run in the park. The late afternoon sunlight is pure gold, and a fresh breeze rustles the tall grass.
A family approaches us on the trail—a man, a woman, and two
small boys. They are accompanied by a large tan dog with the dis-
tended nipples of motherhood and an adorable pup who looks just
like his mom. The pup pesters the older dog, taking five leaping
and bouncing steps for every one of hers. She patiently tolerates
him.

It's a heart-warming scene that depresses me deeply.

What has happened to me? I love dogs. I love puppies. And yet
the sight of puppies saddens me. Every time I see or hear of a litter
of kittens or pups, I can also see the cages full of homeless ones
and the bins full of dead ones at the shelter.

MONDAY

It's 8:00 P.M., time to go home. I walk past the cages in the Stray
Cat Room. A calico cat and her two kittens sit quietly on the shelf
in their cage. The mother grooms one of the kittens. A pink card
attached to the cage tells me it's time to say goodbye to these
three. I feel the all-too-familiar mixture of sadness, anger and bitterness, but I try not to let my emotions show.

A huddled gray ball of fur catches my eye. In the furthest

corner of her cage, a bedraggled cat hides her head under the sheet of newspaper lining her enclosure. I peer between the bars. "Hi, Kitty," I say softly. "Are you totally miserable? I don't blame you." I chatter on, more for my own benefit than for hers. I put some treats into her bowl and leave.

TUESDAY

A small, frightened black rabbit is rescued from a cellar by one of our officers. That evening, in a room full of noisy cats, she gives birth to five babies. Four days later, when her stray holding period is over, the babies are injected with sodium pentobarbitol. A few seconds later, they are dead. The mother is put up for adoption.

Gray Cat clings to her corner, still facing the wall. I notice that she's eaten the treats that I left, which encourages me. I talk to her again. "I know it's hard to believe, but actually you're pretty lucky. Decent food, a clean litter box, people who care about you—and with a little luck, one special person to appreciate and adore you forever." Gray Cat is not impressed.

WEDNESDAY

I talk to the people in my dog-training class about spaying and neutering. "Of the more than 10 million dogs and cats who are killed every year at animal shelters in the U.S., nearly 3 million are purebreds," I explain. "And all the others had a purebred in their recent genetic past. Stand at our front counter any day of the week and you will hear the same stories again and again: 'We're moving'; 'The landlord says no'; 'He barks and the neighbors call the police'; 'She messes in the house.' It doesn't matter if it's a purebred; an expensive pet with a problem is just as disposable as an all-American mutt.

"Spend a day at the shelter and you'll also hear the repertoire of reasons people give for not having their animals spayed or neutered: 'We want the children to experience the miracle of birth'; 'Neutering is unnatural'; 'It's cruel'; 'I wouldn't want anyone to do it to *me*'; 'My cat is from champion stock'; 'We've already got homes lined up for all the babies.' But try to explain these reasons to a loving, beautiful animal—or even an ill-tempered, unlovable one—whose time is up, who is receiving a death sentence when the only crime that has been committed is by a human who allowed the animal to be born, instead of facing the reality of the pet overpopulation disaster. I've never heard a rationalization for not neutering or spaying that didn't just fade into meaninglessness in the face of even just one death."

After class, one of the dog owners comes over to me. "We were planning to let our dog have just one litter," he says, "but we had no idea about how bad the situation really is. We've decided to have her spayed instead." I smile. I feel I've done a good day's work.

On my way out, I stop at Gray Cat's cage again. "Hi, Gray Cat. Still memorizing that bit of wall, I see." She turns and looks at me. Maybe I'm being too optimistic, but she seems a little less frightened, her body a shade more relaxed. "Listen," I tell her, "you probably came across some pretty irresponsible humans out there. We're not all like that. Give us another chance, okay?" She blinks dubiously. This *is* progress.

THURSDAY

The animal care technicians at the shelter are the bravest people in the world. I watch them scrub kennels and clean litter boxes. I hear them try to calm frightened animals. I see them take a moment to play with a kitten or hold a lonely pup. And every now and then I force myself to witness what they must face every day. That same dog who they cared for, petted and talked to must finally be given the only thing we have left to offer: a gentle, respectful death. What have we come to when the best we can do is to kill them kindly?

Jim puts a leash on the Labrador mix. She cowers in the back of the kennel, tail between her legs. He tugs on the leash. She whimpers and crouches down lower. He kneels beside her. "It's okay, pup. Don't be scared." She stops whimpering but won't move. He scoops her up in his arms and carries her to the Euthanasia Room.

She's been at the shelter for two weeks. She's so frightened that all she does is lie in the corner. No one wants her. So now she will die.

Carol holds her while Jim shaves a small patch of fur from one of her front legs. She is quiet and trembling. Jim continues to talk soothingly to her. He gives her the injection. She slumps on the table. Carol carries her body to the "Chill Room" and adds it to the pile.

In the Cat Room, Gray Cat is still in her usual corner, but she's not facing the wall today. The room is noisy. Adorable kittens fill row upon row of cages. Friendly adult cats come forward, asking for attention. When I open her cage to give her a treat, she tenses a little. "It isn't fair," I tell her. "You have every right to distrust people. But if you don't act 'adoptable,' how can you compete with all these other cats?" I reach my hand closer to her. I touch her. She lets me! I thank her.

FRIDAY

At home, someone from a rescue group calls me to find out if I have room for another "unwanted." A local veterinarian has a young Abyssinian cat. The owners brought him in to be euthanized. Why? They're moving out of state. They don't want to take the cat. They haven't found any friend who will take him, and they don't want "a bunch of strangers" coming to their house to see the cat.

When I go to work, Gray Cat is not in her cage. I look everywhere. I try not to be too hopeful. I tell myself not to pursue it. I ignore my own good advice. I go to the Chill Room. She is there, in one of the bins, her body curled up against that of a Golden Retriever. I touch her, for the second and last time. Her body is just now growing cold. She is gone. I will mourn her. But who will mourn the calico kitten underneath her, or the angora rabbit in the next bin? Who will mourn all 10 million of them, one by one?

SATURDAY

I walk through the auditorium. The children's humane education group, Critter Crusaders, meets once a week. They are using recently donated video equipment to make public service announcements about pet overpopulation for local TV stations. As I watch them rehearse their lines about the importance of spaying and neutering, I feel hopeful. They won't forget. They'll tell their friends what they've learned. They'll grow up to teach their own children. I wish Gray Cat were here to see it.

Andrew's Wake

LAURA BEVAN

URRICANES ARE GIVEN human names and the damage they do is often described in terms of human emotions like anger and fury. After spending a month in the south Florida area devastated by Hurricane Andrew in the summer of 1992, I think I know why this is so. It is difficult to observe such massive, incomprehensible destruction without imagining that it was done in a fit of irrational, vengeful rage.

In the early morning of August 24th, Hurricane Andrew smashed into Florida's coast south of Miami. Within a few hours, hundreds of thousands of people lost their jobs, homes, and belongings. Thirty-eight people lost their lives. Hundreds of thousands of animals were killed, injured, or driven from their homes. It was the animals who were the silent victims of Andrew, and their urgent, overwhelming needs consumed my life and the lives of many others for almost two full months.

A day earlier the word had gone out: A tropical storm named Andrew had gained power over the Atlantic and was heading inland with the force of a thousand run-away freight trains. Residents of south Florida mobilized for Andrew's arrival. For pet owners seeking safe haven for their animals, the options available were limited.

Evacuation shelters do not accept any animals, no matter how cherished. To protect a pet, a person must flee with their animal along clogged highways, leave the animal home alone and hope for the best, or stay and try to ride out the storm. Whatever choices people made, no one was adequately prepared for Andrew's devastation.

One man had left his three cats in the bathroom of his mobile home, believing it was the safest place in the house. When he returned home from a disaster shelter, he found *nothing* left—no home, no cats. A month later he was still searching for his cats, hoping that somehow they would miraculously be found. He was only one of many pet owners haunted by the unanswered question of their animal's ultimate fate.

No one will ever know how many animals were lost, injured, or killed in the storm. Horses bolted from stables and fields, dogs and cats fled their homes in terror. Thousands of exotic animals from zoos and private collections were also loose. For days, there was no accurate news on the extent of the damage or displacement, especially regarding animals, so chaos reigned.

When information did start flowing, it was stunning. Thousands of lost, injured, frightened and hungry dogs and cats roamed neighborhoods. It wasn't long before dog packs had formed in many of the most devastated areas. In rural areas hundreds of dead and injured horses lay in the fields. Over 2,000 primates had escaped from zoos and other facilities.

One of the first eye-witness accounts of animal suffering came from Joe Terragrosa, of the South Florida SPCA. Driving his truck and flying in a helicopter over devastated areas, he found horses up to their necks in mud, or in agony from the broken bones and deep gouges caused by storm-thrown, airborne objects. Some animals could be saved, but those beyond hope had to be humanely put down. It was grueling, heart-wrenching work.

Quickly, the communication network among animal-protection and animal-control organizations was activated and put into high gear. The Humane Society of the United States (HSUS), The American Humane Association, and the Florida Animal Control Association all worked together to coordinate their efforts. A team of animal welfare professionals from South Carolina, veterans of Hurricane Hugo relief work, prepared to bring in animal crates, pet food and supplies, and purified water. Calls came in from all over the country offering aid. Large pet food companies responded by donating tens of thousands of pounds of dog and cat food.

We had to determine where the donations would be stored and how they would be distributed to those in need. Some pet food was transferred to the Red Cross food-distribution system. Other food was driven into the damaged areas by volunteers who simply gave it away from the back of their vehicles. Care had to be exercised in the handling and storage of vast quantities of food to prevent spoilage in the humid and damp conditions.

Portable generators were desperately needed to provide basic electricity. South Florida SPCA's Joe Terragrosa carried a generator with him on his daily journeys into the disaster area so he could pump out flooded areas to reach distressed and stranded animals and humans. He was the first person some rural residents had contact with after the storm.

By the weekend two distribution sites had been set up for horse feed, and Tropical Park, a former racetrack, had become both haven and veterinary clinic for severely injured horses. The South Florida SPCA and the Horse Protection Association set up a compound for lost horses five miles north of Homestead, ground zero of the hurricane's worst damage. The number of horses at both sites soon grew to almost 200.

Each day was fraught with unexpected problems. Some of the many primates that were loose had escaped from the University of Miami's research centers; panicky residents, terrified by rumors that the monkeys had AIDS, shot the animals on sight. Horses were being stolen, reportedly by "killer buyers," intending to make some quick money by selling them for slaughter. As quickly as crises arose, solutions had to be found. State authorities and agencies were struggling with a glut of their own problems; it often remained for our network of animal welfare representatives to try to troubleshoot these animal-related problems.

A command center was set up at a local humane society, and then, when it reopened, at a local animal control facility. The devastated region had two veterinary MASH-type facilities to provide emergency care.

Still, more needed to be done. Sally Matluk of Citizen's Against Pet Overpopulation in Fort Lauderdale and I had stopped by the lost horse compound when an idea struck us. As we watched the horses grazing contentedly we wondered if a similar compound couldn't be set up for lost dogs and cats. Up to this point, no central facility existed to house the multitude of lost animals, and there was no single place for anxious pet owners to look for their lost animals. Those who had found animals also needed a place to bring them.

Sally and her husband, John Boisseau, took action. In the late hours of September 4th the Western Small Animal MASH Unit was created. John raided his movie-production company. Suddenly a recreational vehicle, tents, generators and other equipment appeared on the unused front pasture of the lost horse compound. The MASH unit grew rapidly: we added the crates donated by our supporters from South Carolina to house lost dogs and cats, a Coachman travel trailer, and a forty-four-foot tractor-trailer for food storage, courtesy of the Orlando Humane Society.

The U.S. Army's 478th Civil Affairs Battalion lent us three massive army tents to protect the animals and our veterinary clinic from direct sunlight. Soldiers brought food, drinks, and other supplies daily. They watched over all the MASH veterinary clinics at night to prevent looting and vandalism, as volunteers slept in their cars. Many lost and injured companion animals found their way to our compound in army vehicles. One soldier, a M-16 rifle thrown over his shoulder, regularly helped bottle-feed tiny kittens.

Col. Thelton ("Mac") McCorkle, D.V.M., a reservist from the 478th Battalion, and the HSUS' Staff Veterinarian Dr. Steve Kritsick joined forces to serve as the compound's primary veterinarians. They toiled in the heat and humidity to provide whatever medical care they could in less-than-sterile conditions with limited medical supplies. Some days the line of patients snaked through the entire compound. At night, almost like clockwork, soldiers and pet owners arrived at the compound with dogs and cats who had been hit by cars while wandering. In the pitch blackness of the disaster area, a generator pumped enough power to illuminate the makeshift treatment area. Because aggressive dogs were roaming the streets freely and other animals no longer had the protection their fencing had once afforded, many patients with dog bites were also brought in for veterinary care.

After three weeks of fifteen- to eighteen-hour days, I headed back, with some guilt over abandoning my compatriots, to the HSUS Regional Office in Tallahassee to catch up on some other pressing animal issues, which remarkably had not gone away just because of Andrew! After spending a week attending to some urgent matters, I headed back to Homestead. The situation was vastly improved. The compound was operating smoothly, few stray animals remained unclaimed, demand for services was gradually decreasing to a manageable level, and thanks to two airlines which offered special fares, experienced shelter workers from Massachusetts had flown in to relieve fatigued volunteers.

As my last week at the compound progressed, the number of workers slowly diminished. Some had gone as long as a month without pay and needed to return to family and jobs. As life in south Florida began its slow return to normalcy, the life of the compound was nearing its natural end. On my last night there, the giant generator powering the horse and small animal compound imploded. We took it as a final sign that it was time to disband the center.

On October 7 the last dogs left the compound, followed by every trace of its existence. The facility had housed more than 600 dogs and cats at different times and provided veterinary care to an estimated 1,000 or more. Our sister compound for large animals took care of 110 horses, several cows, and a llama.

The animal stories of Andrew could fill a book. There were the tears of joy as a pet thought to be lost forever was found by a grateful owner, and the pained expressions of those who could not care for their pet and had to turn them over to us. Some of these animals went to temporary foster homes, others found new homes.

One hurricane survivor, a sweet, middle-aged beagle-terrier mix, found a new home with me. Two months after Andrew tore her world apart, she is still too frightened to be left alone in the house. When I returned home after leaving her alone the first time, the terror in her eyes sent chills through me. I will never know what she went through during the hurricane, but I hope time and enough love will heal her mental wounds.

Hurricane Andrew taught us many lessons. I learned more than I ever wanted to know about the impact nature's destructive forces can have, and how to assist the animal victims of such a tragedy. Most of all I learned that we must be better prepared for all natural disasters—the animals will depend on it.

This is the Way We Play God

KAREN SHEA

And this is the way we play God
Dumb creatures
Surrendered
By dumb people
Too many animals
Too few homes
Too little time

Caged
They wait
for freedom
the public passes by
blind unaware
it is at fault yet
"What the eyes can't see
The heart can't grieve over"

Stress
Illness
Overcrowding
Prejudice?

The basis for our decision
We have no right

Yet we have no choice
Too many animals
Too few homes
Too little Time

Spring
A beginning
In basket boxes
Surrendered to us
Four eight six
At a time
Spring
An end

Needle shoots through
Fur flesh heart
Of kittens
Not yet able to walk
Never to know
Finer points
Of a feline heritage

Puppies
Too loyal naive
To sleep forever
Never to learn
"Sit"
"Roll over"
"Play dead"
It is not a game
This is the way we play God.

Roundup at Rowdy Creek

DAN LEAVITT

"I'm supposed to remember: All they asked me to do was count them..."

O N OCTOBER 5, 1988, after returning from a short trip out of town, I found a message on my Humane Society of Del Norte County answering machine from the Assistant District Attorney. The Animal Control Department of Del Norte County, a rural county located 350 miles north of San Francisco in the northwest corner of California, had written a citation for dog licensing violations. There was some question as to exactly how many dogs were owned by "Gordon and Catherine Cunningham." The Cunninghams were illegally camped with their dogs on federal forest land about eight miles from Highway 101, up what is known as "Rowdy Creek Canyon." The D.A. wanted to know whether there were thirty of forty dogs. They needed the information for a hearing that was scheduled for October 7th.

Because the dogs were located on federal land, I invited an agent from the California Department of Fish and Game to accompany me. Warden Don Kelly offered to drive, since he had a four-wheel-drive vehicle and I wasn't entirely sure where we were going. The Cunninghams had moved their camp several times. After searching back roads and questioning deer hunters we encountered along the way, we had a general idea of where the dogs and their owners were. Tanker Fill Road was our destination.

About fifty yards down the road, we could hear the dogs barking. Make a left—then a right! Turn here. As we drove in we were greeted by about forty (?) small, terrier-sized dogs. We saw a pickup truck and camper, and a small trailer. As we drove in closer, we could see dogs tied up *everywhere*. There were also numerous dogs running free. Dogs were tied in pairs; some on long chains, some on short. The conditions were terrible. We didn't see any water containers or food bowls. An elderly woman was standing in the midst of all the dogs, with garbage strewn all around her. She was as surprised to see us as we were to see that many dogs in one place. We introduced ourselves, and asked her if the dogs belonged to her. She said yes, they did. We asked her how many dogs she had. She answered that she didn't know—she hadn't counted them lately. There were so many dogs we couldn't even begin to get a "rough" count. It was a hot day—within minutes the stench and the fleas jumping on us through the truck windows became unbearable. We drove down off the mountain and back to town. I was overwhelmed.

The next morning I appeared in court to testify that there were indeed more than thirty dogs, and that the animal neglect and cruelty defied description. The judge ordered that licenses would have to be purchased for the dogs, but that any neglect/cruelty charges would have to be heard at a later date. The D.A. thanked me for taking the census.

The neglect and cruelty I had witnessed was still so fresh in my mind that I knew it had to be stopped as soon as possible. After discussions with the D.A.'s office it was determined that even though the County Animal Control Department had originally made the discovery of the large number of dogs being kept by the Cunninghams some six months earlier (when the couple was told to leave the federal forest land and remove the animals—but only moved down the road), it was time for the Humane Society of Del Norte County to step in and put a stop to the on-going cruelty.

Now what to do? Our humane society had no shelter of its own, limited funds, no paid employees, and I was its only humane officer. County Animal Control had a shelter—with room for only twenty-seven dogs—but it was full. I would need supplies, help with the collection of evidence, and assistance impounding the dogs. I called upon friends in the field and they came through with generous support. Pat Miller of the Marin Humane Society—over five hours and 300 miles away—sent State Humane Officer Captain Cindy Machado, who brought with her a fully equipped truck, animal ID bands, a 35mm camera, and a video camera. The cavalry had arrived!

Prior to Cindy's arrival I had contacted the county fairgrounds manager and arranged for the use of the compound's horse barn to temporarily house the dogs. I also contacted a local veterinarian so he would be ready for the arrival of the dogs. I was certain the dogs would have plenty of medical problems that would need immediate attention.

On the morning of October 10th, after unsuccessfully attempting to obtain a search warrant (it was a holiday and no judge was available), Captain Machado, County Animal Control Officer George Alexander, California Highway Patrol Officer Rick Stovall, one Sheriff's reserve deputy, and the editor of the local paper and I caravaned up the mountain. After some discussion, we had concluded that since the camp was on federal land, a warrant wasn't necessary.

The conditions at the camp were worse than I remembered. Dogs chained near each other were so entangled that they could not move. No dogs had water containers. Dog food was seen near some of the entangled dogs, but it was out of their reach. Accumulated dog feces covered the entire camp. The majority of dogs had no shelter from the elements. It was eighty degrees, and there was only partial shade. The dogs who were chained had the chains clasped around their necks with no collars or swivels. Some dogs were so weak they couldn't stand. There were four or five female dogs with puppies located in a closed camp trailer. Dog feces from two to six inches deep covered the counters and floor of the trailer. There was no water.

Mrs. Cunningham was at the campsite; her husband was not. I informed her that we were impounding all of the dogs under numerous violations of section 597PC of the Penal Code—Crimes Against Animals. I explained that she had the choice of signing a surrender statement turning over all the dogs to us. Miraculously, she signed it.

Now the "fun" began. Imagine trying to round up over one hundred dogs, the majority of whom have never been handled by anyone. We attempted to catch, tag, and systematically catalog all the dogs. After about dog number thirty, we realized we would run out of daylight long before we ran out of dogs. At that point we began to load them into trucks according to size, planning to tag and catalog them after we got off the mountain. In the process, we were all nipped at least once (nothing serious). Mrs. Cunningham helped load the more unpredictable adult dogs, and even she was bitten.

We returned to town with three vehicles filled to capacity with dogs. It took an additional trip to get the rest of the pack. We brought sixty-eight more dogs down on the second trip. It was dark when we arrived at the horse barns and unloaded the second group. Two were taken to the veterinary clinic immediately, but they were so malnourished and dehydrated that they couldn't be saved.

Captain Machado's job was done. Mine was just beginning. With a sinking feeling I watched as she drove away into the night, headed back home. I now had the responsibility of caring for over one hundred unsocialized, frightened, neglected dogs. Thank God for the efforts of our humane society's volunteers, who helped with this incredible task while we waited for the wheels of justice to turn.

The final head count was 129 dogs. We had dogs housed in fifteen box stalls. It wasn't the best, but it was all we had, and it was unquestionably better than where they had been. We soon found that putting their dog food in containers was impossible. The dogs fought over every morsel of food. Even young puppies would lay on pieces of dog food and growl as they ate. We finally found that broadcasting the food like we were feeding chickens was the only way to keep them from fighting over it. After a few days, the dogs began to realize that there was plenty of food (thanks to donations from a local supermarket), and they became less frenzied, even leaving some food to eat later.

It was a lot of work for an all-volunteer agency unaccustomed to sheltering large numbers of animals. We would get through feeding, cleaning and watering the dogs just in time to start over again. At first, many of the dogs sat huddled in a corner when we entered the stalls. The ones we could pick up simply froze, and remained motionless while being held. As the vet examined them and we began to tag them, we started making notes about their behavior, and which ones might be adoptable. Each day our volunteers sat with many of the dogs and worked on socializing them. Each day more and more of them began to show trust, and warmed up to their rescuers. The dogs were dirty, flea-bitten, and their coats were matted. By the end of one week, with the help of a local groomer and a number of volunteers, all forty-seven adoptable dogs had been cleaned up. Unfortunately, many of the adult dogs had been unsocialized for far too long. Given the opportunity they would function like a mini-wolf pack, ready to attack as a unit.

Deciding which animals will be euthanized is always the difficult part of this job. For the Cunningham dogs it was tragic. Due to the aggressive and untrustworthy nature of many of the dogs, and the assorted chronic health problems, sixty adult dogs and twenty unweaned pups had to be euthanized. It was one of the hardest decisions I have ever had to make.

After being socialized by a local 4-H group, eleven of the dogs were adopted out in Del Norte County. The remainder were transported to the Humboldt Humane Society, the Marin Humane Society, the Peninsula Humane Society, and Haven Humane Society. All were placed in homes.

Of the many things this case taught me, perhaps the most important is that even though I work alone as the only Humane Officer in a large, rural county, one phone call brought me the expertise, support and assistance of animal welfare professionals from other communities who were more than willing to assist. Alone, the challenges seem overwhelming; together we can face even the biggest ones, as we did with the Cunningham dogs.

POSTSCRIPT: The Cunninghams were charged with nine separate county, state, and federal criminal violations. They were found guilty on all but one count. They were each sentenced to ten days in jail, with their fine, probation and physical ability to serve jail time to be determined at a subsequent hearing. They and their attorney failed to appear at the hearing; a no-bail warrant was issued for their arrest.

Gone to the Beach

DIANE W. LECRONE

I drove on out to the shelter today
    to purchase some Science Diet,
I saw no cars in the parking lot
    and it was amazingly quiet.

I stepped from my car and,
    with the door within reach,
I read the scribbled note which said,
    "Gone to the beach."

The handwritten note was
    from all of the staff,
And as I read further,
    I just had to laugh.

Since all owners of pets
    had them neutered or spayed,
This day that we'd dreamed of
    and hoped for and prayed,

Had finally come,
    so I stepped inside.
The cages were empty
    the gates opened wide.

The goal had been reached,
   all the pets had a home.
No more cruelty to see
   no more strays on the roam.

Literally jumping for joy
   and letting out a scream,
I started myself
   from this wonderful dream.

So it wasn't true,
   but it's not too late,
If your pet's not sterile—
   call the vet, set a date.

If we all do our part
   by stopping the chain,
of carelessly breeding,
   then hope will remain.

For the shelter staff would
   be truly overjoyed,
on the day they can say
   we are unemployed.

The Night Before Christmas, Shelter-Style

PAT MILLER

'Twas the week before Christmas, and
    all thru the shelter
Staff was having parties; work was done
    helter-skelter.
The cookies were placed in the kitchen
    with care,
With hopes the dogs wouldn't get
    to them there.

The critters were nestled all snug in their
    beds,
While visions of new owners danced in
    their heads.
Diane in her blue jeans and Pam, smiling
    hearty,
Were sitting down to plan just one
    more party

When out in the front there arose such
    a clatter
We sprang from our desks to see what
    was the matter!
Cindy jumped from her chair to the
    door in a flash

Praying Officer Sue hadn't had one more
crash.

The sun on the parking lot's new fallen
rain
Made it clear that "Lake Sumner" still
failed to drain,
When what to our wondering eyes
should appear,
But a miniature sleigh, and eight tiny
reindeer.

While Tom checked for permits and
Steve wrote a cite,
Lynn added up fees for their stay over-
nite.
Donna looked through our request files
with gloom,
While Kim cleaned the barn out and
tried to make room.

Judy called me and said "Get out front
on the double,
There's a weird man out there; I think
this means trouble."
I stepped out and saw a right jolly old
elf;
And I laughed when I saw him, in spite
of myself

His eyes how they twinkled! His laughter, how merry!
His cheeks were like roses, his nose like
a cherry.

A stub of a pipe he held clenched in his
   teeth,
And the smoke it encircled his head like
   a wreath.

'Til Trish marched to the counter and
   said with a sneer,
"I'm sorry, we don't allow smoking in
   here…"
I made my approach with a great deal
   of speed
And said, "Can I help you? Is there
   something you need?"

"I'm starting my rounds, and checking
   my list.
I'm trying to grant the humane workers'
   wish;
No more suffering and pain for all the
   world's critters,
A good home for each pet, and lots
   fewer litters."

"I'm sorry I can't do it all in one day,
But thanks to you all, this much I can
   say:
If you keep up the outstanding work
   that you do,
One of these days, your dreams will
   come true."

So saying, he turned and walked out the
   door,

And I knew that we would see him no
  more.
Still I heard him exclaim, as he drove
  out of sight,
"Happy Christmas to all creatures, and
  to all a good life!"

Firestorm Diary

KATHY NASH

EDITOR'S NOTE: *Humane society personnel are often dispatched to help neighboring agencies when the demands of a large cruelty case or natural disaster exceed a local organization's resources. Such was the case when California's devastating Oakland Hills Fire struck in 1991. Officers and volunteers were sent from humane societies throughout Northern California to assist the City of Oakland's Animal Control Department and the Oakland SPCA. The following is a diary of one of the volunteer rescue workers.*

12:00 A.M.

It is midnight and I can't sleep. For animals whose world is governed by the senses, those that survived face alien territory. Nothing is the same. Their homes no longer stand, their eyes and lungs burn from the smoke, the constant rumble of large trucks and helicopters overhead add to the animals' fear. Some, having fled, may be far from their original homes, and walking is painful on burned feet. Terrified, they hide quietly under slabs of concrete, fallen walls and skeletons of automobiles—instinct and fear may keep them hiding and unapproachable for days or weeks.

6:15 A.M.

In pursuit of the orange tabby, one of our officer's started up a steep hill. The burned cat moved slowly. Under normal conditions, it would have been easy to rescue him. But the terrain made it impossible for Tom to move quickly, and the cat escaped after a lengthy, although very slow, chase. From the bottom of the hill, Tom's khaki uniform blended into the charred terrain—when he disappeared from sight, I worried about him as well as the cat.

9:30 A.M.

As we entered the apartment complex, we were flagged down by police officers who led us to the raccoon. He was moving up a hill on painfully burned legs. It took almost half an hour with the raccoon determined to outwit the officers. With the help of a police officer, Tom finally captured the still feisty animal. He was taken to the wildlife rehabilitation center. I don't know if he made it.

10:05 A.M.

A few yards away, I stooped down, trying to reach another raccoon—this one dead and floating in a pool. Unable to reach the body, I turned to stand up. Peering solemnly at me from the bushes was a tiny black-and-white tuxedo kitten. Only the rustle of the burned leaves gave his position away. A quiet approach, and a few words of kitten baby-talk later, the little guy was purring in my arms. Ravenous, he gobbled down lunch as I marvelled that something so tiny and fragile had survived.

1:00 P.M.

After a fire, there is no real color, just black, white and brown. Singed fur perfectly camouflaged the animals we were trying to find, and the rubble provided millions of hiding places for small pets. Only the blink of an eye or the flick of a tail alerted us to survivors. Burned-out trees, still hot to the touch, loose sliding dirt, rubble and the steep terrain slows our progress; every step must be calculated to avoid tripping or falling.

2:20 P.M.

He was spotted by an alert humane officer under a slab of concrete. It took six people and four nets to bring the beautiful Lynx Point Siamese to safety. Fighting and terrified, she was placed in a carrier and taken back to the shelter. The next morning I found her calm and purring, and by afternoon she had been claimed by her overjoyed owner.

4:10 P.M.

Officer Snyder saw the badly burned cat, the slightest hint of motion the only indication she was still alive. Lying against the foundation, she was unable to stand, and barely conscious. Unfortunately, she was conscious enough to feel the pain. Third degree burns over half her body, ears almost burned off, eyes burned closed and lungs damaged, there was no hope for this little tortie. Humane euthanasia was authorized and her pain ended. Our pain lingers in the knowledge that there are probably so many more suffering that will not be found in time.

5:25 P.M.

A block away we were stopped by a young woman searching for her two cats. Her home had been destroyed, but she was remarkably composed because there was something of more value to search for—her pets. A few minutes later, standing in the rubble that had been her living room, we found the tiny remains of one cat. All I could do was hold her and hug her as we both cried.

7:45 P.M.

Panicked, the Siamese had bitten and scratched his owner who tried to rescue him. Now the cat picked his way up the hill. Officer Snyder followed. His face almost parallel to the steep hill, he couldn't see the cat. We navigated for him from below, hoping the cat would give up, or turn back towards the nets we had waiting. No luck—the cat disappeared over the ridge. Disappointed, Paul had to carefully slide back down the hill.

On a normal, good day a search for missing animals can be difficult and time-consuming. In this disaster, everything ran against us: inaccessible roads, waits behind rescue and repair vehicles, dangerous rubble sliding beneath our feet and no landmarks to go by in an area with which we were not familiar. It is a miracle any animals were found and rescued. It was tedious, tiring and depressing work, followed by tears and sleepless nights. But no one considered even for a moment that it wasn't worth it—even if we were responsible for saving only a few animals out of thousands who were displaced by the fire.

The Little Red Hound That Could

NANCY P. RICHARDS

THE HUMANE SOCIETY of Southeast Missouri was only one of many shelters in the Midwest affected by the flooding of the Mississippi in the summer of 1993. We were lucky in the sense that our facility was quite a distance from the actual flood waters. Still, as the river's waters continued to rise, we knew we had to prepare ourselves for another kind of flood—this one of animals. As more and more people lost their homes there would be ever-increasing numbers of displaced animals in need of care. We quickly mobilized, setting up foster homes, contacting veterinarians who could be on stand-by to provide care for sick and injured animals, and alerting local disaster assistance agencies about the aid we could offer animal owners.

It was in the midst of this preparation that I received a call on August 10th from a Red Cross official. He had just returned from the small town of Thebes, Illinois, where there was a family that had "drowning cats and dogs in their basement." Less than a few seconds after getting the necessary information and dropping the phone, I flew out the door armed with boots, pet carriers, gloves and anything else I could think of that would help. Thebes was only about twenty miles away, but the drive seemed to last forever as my mind raced with images of trapped animals struggling to stay afloat. I finally reached my destination. Mrs. R., the homeowner (her name has been abbreviated to protect her privacy), anxiously shook her head. "No, no, they're not in my basement—they're trapped on my farm. It's only a few miles down the road, but we'll have to take my boat to get there…"

Mrs. R. was a small, frail woman in her sixties. Her face had the weathered look of many years of hard work. Her husband, who had Alzheimer's Disease, sat in a chair in the front yard staring blankly ahead. Natural disasters do not choose their victims. Still, I couldn't help feeling anger over the fact that people who have already suffered enough misfortune in life would have to weather an additional crisis like this.

Mrs. R. started up her old station wagon and I followed in our shelter van. We drove down several narrow gravel roads until we reached her boat. I had seen countless rescues over the last month on TV by the Coast Guard in their high-powered, well-equipped motorboats. Imagine my surprise when Mrs. R.'s boat turned out to have *no* engine. The next thing I knew she was handing me a paddle. "We only have to row about half a mile to get there," she said. We loaded some carriers and food from the van into the small craft, and were ready to go. I put on my boots and waded into the filthy, stagnant water to push the boat off, realizing too late that I had grabbed the leaky pair of boots! Soon we were off and paddling though, with Mrs. R. pointing out things along the way, and sadly remarking, "That used to be…"

After forty-five minutes of dodging tree branches and debris and swatting away countless bugs, we finally reached an old farmhouse with flood waters up to its front porch. As I slowly scanned the area, I noticed what looked like a small island behind the house. As we moved closer, I began to hear barking, and there, on the only ground that remained above water, were cats, chickens, ducks, roosters, and several large dogs, obviously happy to see us. Before we could even get out of the boat, two of the dogs had jumped in, nearly knocking us backward into the water! Mrs. R.

told me the dogs were all strays that she had been feeding. Just one glance told me that I was dealing with dogs afflicted with a variety of health problems, including mange, ringworm, fleas, and probably other parasites too.

We had little time to waste, as the flood waters were continuing to rise. Mrs. R. fed the fowl, while I started packing cats in carriers. One of the cats—a pretty little tortoise-shell—had just had kittens the day before. I gently packed her and her five babies in one of the travel kennels. We realized that we would only be able to take one of the dogs with us on the first trip—the boat was too small to hold more. Soon we were ready to leave with eleven cats and one very restless thirty pound dog in my lap. As we pushed off, rowing the boat proved to be extremely difficult. As I tried to hold the dog still and row at the same time, I heard a loud splash. It was the largest of the dogs we had left behind swimming towards us. We turned around and headed back to the farmhouse, where he heaved his massive body out of the water and up onto the porch, and then straight into the boat, landing on top of me and the dog in my lap! I was sure we were going to tip, but somehow we regained our balance. We breathed a sigh of relief, and, determining that we could handle the weight of the additional dog (which actually helped to balance our boat's load), we left again.

Mid-way back to where we had left the station wagon and van, I heard a soft, lapping noise. Turning around, I stared in disbelief, as another one of the dogs, this one a small red hound, was paddling as hard as she could trying to reach us. After a frantic but unsuccessful search for a place to stop and pull her in, we painfully realized she would have to swim the rest of the way. We rowed as fast and hard as we could, struggling to keep from being capsized by the excited dogs, and continually yelling shouts of encouragement to the little red hound trailing behind.

Finally, the vehicles were in view and we were soon able to bring the boat safely up on the shore that was once a road. Even getting *out* of the boat with all the animals was no easy task, but soon everyone was safely on land, including the little red hound. She was exhausted. I carried her to the van first, then loaded everyone else. Hot, wet, tired, and bleeding from scratches from tree branches and the animals, Mrs. R. and I rested against the van for a moment. Since the animals left behind had been fed and watered, and it would soon be dark, we decided to meet the next morning to retrieve them.

As I drove the van back to the shelter, I glanced into the rearview mirror frequently to check on my tired crew. Although exhausted, I smiled to myself, relieved that we had been successful in our mission.

The next day proved as harrowing and exhausting as the first, but soon everyone was safely at the shelter. Several of the cats and kittens were placed in foster care, and eventually adopted into loving homes. Sadly, none of the dogs were as lucky. They had advanced cases of mange, they had all tested positive for heart-worm, and they were afflicted with a variety of other chronic health problems. Despite our efforts, it was too late for them.

I will never forget the little red hound though, who was so determined not to be left behind that she ventured into filthy, dangerous waters, and courageously swam to catch up with us. And I will never forget the remarkable Mrs. R. who continued to row out to the island every day for weeks to feed her chickens and ducks, until the flood waters eventually receded. Her perseverance and commitment to her animals, as well as all the other animals who were not as fortunate during the Flood of 1993, will always remain with me.

A Day in the Life

WARD P. STERLING

I T'S MY FRIDAY; TO EVERYONE else a Saturday. The day starts out slow. I get into my truck and pull away from the shelter, pointing the hood toward my beat area for the day: Daly City and Pacifica. I think of 4:30 P.M., when I'll get to go home for my weekend.

My first stop is at a familiar house; the dog there has caused quite a problem, bitten a few people. The dog owner isn't going to get the dog back until he builds a proper fence. He's a bit resistant, but he finally understands.

Next stop is an abandonment complaint. A neighbor says the dog's owner was evicted a few days ago but that their dog is still at the house. The neighbor is tired of the howling; the dog is probably lonely. The eviction notice on the front door makes it obvious that no one is home except the mature, long-haired male Collie.

In my experience, a dog that's been left behind isn't always welcoming, but this one is very friendly. He has a little food left, and the water is turning green, but he will be okay. Our usual procedure in this situation is to give a time limit and, after twenty-four hours, impound the dog.

I leave the usual notes taped up in plain view, and as I am about to pull away the radio says my next call is at the same address I am about to leave. The property owner has called and requested that we pick up the dog. I'm happy; now I can really get to meet this beautiful, large, Lassie-like dog. He's wonderful, with only a few mats in his coat that will have to be brushed out.

I tear down the notes and leave a different one. I check the box on the note that says, "YOUR ANIMAL HAS BEEN IMPOUNDED"—as if the person who "YOUR" is aimed at will ever read it.

My next stop is a feral cat in an humane trap who is very scared. In the truck I quickly cover it with darkness to keep it calm and quiet.

Next is a dead raccoon in someone's front yard, probably hit by a car.

Next stop is a dog bite quarantine. Everything is usual. The owner shows me proof of rabies vaccination, and the dog has a current license. I explain the ten-day, in-home quarantine, and ask the owner to notify us if the dog becomes sick, injured, is lost, or dies.

I climb back into the truck, and now the dispatcher has a fevered pitch in his voice—before he even tells me what the call is, I know it is important. A traffic hazard—a stray dog on a busy street. The police are on the scene. Upon my arrival, the dog is frightened and won't come to anyone. So I follow her home, but no one comes to the front door. A bit of chatter on the radio, and out of the corner of my eye I see the side door of the house close. Someone is home, but won't answer the door.

The police are familiar with the house from several previous arrests. With a confirmation of a felony warrant, I'm now backing up the police inside the house. The dog's owner is handcuffed. He tells me to take the dog, but it belongs to a friend that he lost contact with a month-and-one-half ago. He says he can't control the dog, and after an hour of trying, another officer and I can't either. About half way through this ordeal, the dispatcher tells me he has an injured animal waiting. Could be a bird or a dog, I don't know yet. So I leave this problem with the other officer, and take off in my truck.

It's a dog, and he's in bad shape. I get there and find there are actually two dogs. One is seizuring, lying on his left side. All his muscles are strung tight, legs outstretched. The other dog is sitting on a lawn, watching. I quickly impound the healthy one, so I won't lose her. She has a license on, so I quickly jot down the number. I run to the injured dog, who is still seizuring. Quick examination—no open wounds. "I say "Hi, buddy, bad day, huh?" He was staring off into space until then. As I finish my question, he looks at me with his eyes—he can't move his head—and he wags his tail. I almost die—this dog is in such terrific pain and he still wants to wag his tail for me, a complete stranger. I quickly place him in the truck. He has a license too, one digit off from the first dog, obviously owned by the same person. The dog's only chance is a fast trip to the emergency veterinarian. I arrive at the clinic in a hurry, open the kennel compartment, and my heart drops in my chest. The dog is dead.

In the truck the Collie, who has been a little noisy all morning, is now quiet. I wonder if it was the trip down the freeway, or if he understands what has just happened in the kennel next to him.

The next call is a stray Pit Bull, back in Daly City. When I get there, the person who called says the owner came and got the dog.

Time to inhale some food. Through the drive-thru and into a parking lot for a quick ten-minute meal.

My last call is a confined, stray, unweaned kitten. I already know its fate. These guys need to be bottle-fed every few hours. Considering the time involved, and how many unweaned kittens there are…it rides in front with me and I cuddle it and look at its innocent face on the way back to the shelter. I'm glad it doesn't know. I hold it while the animal care technician injects the blue fluid. The kitten takes its final nap in my arms.

I sit down in the squad room to make one last call. A woman answers and I tell her who I am. She's elated. She has been driving around the neighborhood, frantically trying to find her two dogs. "You have them!" I reply "Yes," and carefully add, "but…" After I explain, the woman is very distraught and says she will be down to the shelter shortly. She redeems the healthy dog, and with as composed a face as she can muster, tells me she wants to see the other dog's body.

If there is ever a time in this job when I don't know what to do, it's now. She's crying and talking to the dead dog, and I do my best to console her, but nothing I can say can bring back her friend, or ease her pain.

I get in my personal truck and pull away from the shelter, pointing my hood towards home and my weekend. It's 6:15 P.M. Somehow, I can never seem to get out of there on time.

Against All Odds

JENNIFER SOTELO

Sometimes when I'm walking dogs with prospective adopters, the client will fall silent, look out through the fence at the tombstones north of our shelter, and say, "Is that a pet cemetery? How sad." I don't always say what I am thinking: that there is nothing sad about the little graveyard because the animals who are buried there were wanted animals, whose owners cared enough to memorialize them. If the handful of markers in that plot represented all of the animals who had ever been euthanized at the Humane Society, *that* would be cause for celebration.

What is sad is the number of animals who die every day at the shelter, whose bodies are burned in our crematory, whose ashes are shoveled out and tossed in the dumpster, who become statistics on a piece of paper, their names forgotten or never known.

Many people don't understand that euthanasia is performed by staff members right here at the shelter every day. Some people know and don't care. Others are unable to see us as protectors and friends of animals because of what we are forced to do. If only these people could work here for a summer; clean kennels with our leaky hoses; feed the stray dogs whose ribs stand out like fence railings under their skin; nurse infant kittens with milk in a syringe; drive injured animals to our clinic for evaluation, and if they're lucky, treatment; watch animals being given up from homes because they are too playful or hungry; comfort animals as they come by the truck and van load...if they could only see what we see, we wouldn't have to defend ourselves. If every one knew what we know, they would sterilize their animals and give them the best of care. They would change the truth we have to tell.

Every day we walk past rows of cages, past many pairs of eyes. Most are friendly, some are wide with fear, some glazed with sickness, but all are filled with hope and the desire to live. As we go to sleep at night we can still see them watching us.

A few weeks ago a co-worker and I euthanized a litter of four kittens and their mother. The mother was too wild to be adopted; the kittens too sick to receive foster care from our volunteer foster parents. We tried to make the kittens' deaths as painless as possible. We use an injection of barbiturate, sodium pentobarbitol, which causes unconsciousness and stops the heart beating within seconds after entering the bloodstream. Still, the little ones cried out at the needle prick to their abdomens. A kitten at five-weeks-old fits easily into the palm of one hand. The head is rounded, ears slightly off to the sides. I had foster kittens that age at home whose favorite game was to shimmy up the leg of my jeans right to my hip. As we arranged the little bodies on the table in a row to listen for heartbeats it didn't help to know that they were unadoptable. Someone abandoned them. For this there are no excuses; there is no rationale.

A staff euthanasia support group was created in response to our need to talk about these kinds of experiences. The group provides an opportunity for those of us who perform euthanasia to talk to-gether, to grieve, and to find ways to cope with the hardest part of our job. Our facilitator became involved with the Humane Society when she brought her own dog to us to be euthanized due to old age. She now donates her counseling services to us. She listens carefully and asks simple, provocative questions which help us explore and cope with the feelings we have about the work we do.

At the beginning of the second session of our support group, someone put a box of tissues on a chair in the center of the room. It was a humorous gesture, but by the end of the session none of us could stop the tears from coming. We talked about the animals we had become attached to, only to return to work to find their cage empty, the dog or cat euthanized, and no one to blame. We talked about the abuse and neglect, our anger at the people who know their animals are in pain but fail to care for them. Instead they bring them to us when the animals are in such poor condition that all we can do is put them out of their misery. We talk about trying to maintain our human vulnerability even as we try to toughen ourselves to go on.

Our facilitator encourages us to find strategies for hope and healing. Some of us return to our other duties after a morning of putting animals to sleep and find something nurturing to do for those who remain—like putting a pack on a dog's wound, or administering fluids to a dehydrated cat. Sometimes the staff will rally around a particular animal who has been at the shelter longer than the others—a dog or cat who becomes symbolic of what is possible here. We get the sense if *that* animal can be adopted, anyone—and perhaps someday everyone—can.

I had just started working at the shelter when Rambo, an eight-year-old brown and white mixed-breed dog, who had been in the kennels for four months, found a home. At the time I didn't quite understand why everyone was so ecstatic over the good fortune of a rather funny-looking guy. He has been back to visit us many times with his new owners. I now understand why it is so inspiring to see the simple act of a dog like Rambo bouncing across the parking lot with his owners in tow. He is healthy, happy and loved—a sign of victory over the odds, a symbol of our triumphs.

Shelter Stories

ANNE SPEAKMAN

THE VAN PULLED SLOWLY up to our shelter building. I looked out and saw three children with noses planted against the window. Were they coming to adopt their first puppy? I hoped so. It was the beginning of summer, and we had so many. A woman was out in the parking lot putting a leash on large bouncing dog on the other side of the van. As she walked him to our door, he jumped with anticipation. He was ready to play. No adoption this time. She came in the office and filled out the papers to relinquish the dog. The family was moving to New Jersey.

The dog's name was Nike (like the shoe). Her youngest had found him a few years earlier. He was a good dog—loved kids, etc. But he would be just too much trouble to move along with all the children. They would just find another dog once they got settled. The papers were signed and they left.

I watched the van pull out of the shelter lot. The window was down on the van and out of it came a little tow-headed boy with tears streaming down his little red cheeks. He cried out with hurt so big it tore my heart apart, "I'll come back and get you some day, Nike, I'll come back...."

I turned and headed to the back of the shelter. I gave Nike a little pat on the head as I passed his run. He didn't understand and

I couldn't explain why he was there or the terrible pain I felt for him and his little blond friend.

Inmates—trustees from the county jail—work each day at our shelter. They help clean, feed, and exercise the animals. Many have come and gone over the years, but Tony, the first inmate who worked for us, remains a dear friend, and comes to visit often.

He had been sentenced to ten years hard labor under the Habitual Offenders Act. He had abused drugs and alcohol, and he had been convicted of many crimes. But his life was changed, he told us, because of the shelter, and the things he saw and learned there.

While he worked for us he became attached to one dog in particular. He was a black Husky-mix, with translucent blue eyes. Old Blue Eyes was "his" dog, and Tony loved him. When there was time, Tony, a "hardened criminal," would take Blue Eyes for walks in the nearby woods. He really wanted to find the dog a home. Being locked up wasn't much of a life—this Tony knew.

Months passed and no home was found. We had talked about putting Blue Eyes to sleep. Tony came in to work a few days after we had discussed it. He looked as though he had been crying and his heart was heavy. We talked as we worked. He had come to a decision about "his" dog. It was time to set him free. Tony held Blue Eyes as we injected the lethal solution into his vein. The dog's head dropped as life left him. He lay limp in Tony's arms.

Tony carried his friend into the woods they had walked in and buried him under an old oak tree. He came back to the shelter afterwards, his eyes red and swollen. "It ain't no life to be locked up, even for a dog. I did what was right, I know I did."

Blue Eye's end was a beginning for Tony. After he finished his prison sentence, he married and bought a farm. The unwanted dog

with the translucent blue eyes did not die in vain—he taught a
man about living and changed his life.

There were people who turned in their adolescent animals because
"they'd gotten too big." They were Christmas puppies and kittens
doing the natural thing—growing up. There were those who told
me they "had too many." They had not spayed their female dog or
cat, but they had found homes for her first, second, third, fourth
and even fifth litters. Now they had decided to keep one of her offspring, and bring *her* to the shelter. The list of reasons goes on.
The surrender cards list the litany of reasons: "don't want," "too
many," "too much trouble," "can't keep," "won't stay home,"
"chews," "barks," "too protective," "not protective enough," "in
heat," "pregnant," "moving," "too big," and on and on and
on…"You won't kill them will you?" We are silent. Then we say
that speech, "just so many homes…too many…if people would spay
and neuter…." They turn and walk away. Their conscience is
clear. The responsibility is now ours. Each animal is unique,
trusting, and loving. We feed them, care for them, talk to them,
and then we must end their lives. They have been betrayed.

Penny's Shine

JOAN MARGALITH

WE DON'T KNOW MUCH about Penny's first three
months of life. All we know is that when she was
brought to our shelter hospital, she was one pitiful
pup. Penny's owner had brought her in after a large
truck tire had fallen on her and crushed her right rear leg.

Penny was rushed to the treatment room. While the doctors
were examining her broken leg, they realized that this was not her
only malady. A mean-looking discharge was coming out of her
nose. Her stomach was severely bloated. A gash in her right ear
had been sewn up crudely with coarse, non-sterile stitches and was
badly infected. On top of everything else, Penny's naturally fluffy
coat was covered with grease and dirt. And strangest of all, her
whiskers appeared burnt.

Shelter medical staff X-rayed the injured leg, which was
hanging ominously behind her. There were two serious fractures
and a slight dislocation. They set the leg and put it in a cast. Then
they removed the homemade stitches from Penny's ear, cleaned it
thoroughly, carefully applied new sutures and wrapped it with a
fresh dressing. A fecal examination showed that she had worms, so
she was given medication to eradicate the parasites. And Penny
was put on a special diet suitable for a delicate puppy with intestinal distress.

The next day, Penny's owner came to the hospital expecting to take her home. But Penny had spent a difficult night. Two doctors explained to Penny's owner that her life would be in danger if she left the hospital now. They assured him he shouldn't worry about the expense, because the shelter had a special fund that could assist with the costs of her emergency care.

But that was not what Penny's owner wanted to hear. He had brought her to the shelter's hospital only for her hurt leg and now he wanted her back. The doctors, however, insisted on keeping Penny, and asked for more information about her other problems. At this point, the man began describing, in horrifying details, how he had taken care of his pet.

Penny was subsisting on a diet of nothing but onions, because her owner thought this would "de-worm" her. After the pup had received a cut on her ear (how this happened he couldn't remember), the gash had become infected. Rather than taking her to a veterinarian, he simply tried repairing the problem himself, sewing up the wound with fishing line. As for the discharge from her nose, well, he decided that Penny had distemper. Moreover, he had "cured" the disease. First, he held the pup upside down to let her nose drain. When that didn't work, he inserted an object up her nose to clean out the congestion. Finally, he held Penny over an open flame to clear her breathing passages.

The doctors listened to the man's story with alarm. Based on a very misguided notion of "home care," Penny had been subjected to one torture treatment after another. It was clear to the doctors that they were dealing with a confused person who represented a danger to animals. They notified the shelter's humane officer. The man was subsequently arrested and charged with cruelty to animals, and is now awaiting trial.

With her owner arrested, Penny became a ward of our shelter. Her first twelve weeks of life may have been miserable, but she had just lived through her first full day kindness, with many more to follow. Weak as she was, Penny glowed with kindness.

Penny's next two weeks were spent quietly in the infirmary—healing, resting and gaining weight. The infirmary and shelter staff attended to her needs. They gave her medication. They gently changed her dressings. They kept up her special nutritive diet. And they petted her, talked to her, scratched her tummy, and stroked her fur. They paid a great deal of attention to Penny, giving her something she probably hadn't had so far in her short life—tender, loving care.

Two weeks later, Penny wasn't yet ready for adoption, but she was ready to move in with a foster parent, where she could continue her recovery in a home atmosphere. A woman named Mary had heard about the shelter's foster care program and thought helping an animal in need would be just the thing to help her get through a difficult time of her own. She had fallen and broken a vertebra several months earlier and was still home recuperating—so she had plenty of time to spend with an ailing animal. When Mary heard about Penny, she knew she wanted to open up her home to this dog. Taking care of Penny would take her mind off some of her own troubles, and offer her the opportunity to give Penny some much-needed love.

Mary brought Penny home, a small ball of fluff with a very big cast. The quiet little puppy who still couldn't walk was frightened and worried—for about one day. After that, Penny "came into her own and ruled the roost, playing with everything in sight. She was just plain adorable," says her foster parent, who gave her all her medications, played with her and brought her in to the infirmary every week for check-ups and dressing changes.

Penny's health flourished during her foster care. The shelter continued to provide Penny's medical care and monitor her progress. After two more weeks, Penny's cast came off. And a week later, Penny's fostering phase was over. In just three weeks, she had almost doubled in size and weight. She was now entering the "home stretch." Penny was ready for a permanent place in the heart and home of a loving family.

Picture Penny sitting pretty in her kennel with only two slight scars to show for her history. It was hard to imagine that this enthusiastic, bright-eyed pup had experienced such a sordid past.

It was during this time that Louisa came to the shelter. She had raised many dogs, but her last canine companion had died four years earlier. Now, Louisa was finally ready to take the plunge again. She took her time going through the kennels, looking at every dog. She double- and triple-checked all the dog runs, but there was no doubt in her mind—her destiny was with that adorable pup. Louisa talked with an adoption counselor about this special dog and was more than prepared to attend to her needs. So Penny walked through the same doors she had been carried through only six weeks before. But now she was as proud as she had once been pathetic.

Love wasn't completely blind in this case. Louisa could see Penny's scars and could tell the young dog had been through some rough times. "But," she says, "I knew that would only make her that much more appreciative for the home we wanted to give her. And it's true. Penny is loyal, protective, smart, beautiful, healthy, endearing, easy to train and carefree." Louisa can go on forever singing the praises of her family's new companion. "She's a great family dog. Her instincts around children, adults and other animals are wonderful. She might have a physical scar or two, but there are no scars on her personality whatsoever."

Penny has grown up to be a medium-sized Doberman/Shepherd mix, "a little bit of this and a little bit of that," Louisa says, "...an SPCA special." Louisa goes on to say that, "Penny is leading a very pampered life. She's a great dog and she deserves it."

So that's Penny's story. If you pass her on the street, you might not even notice her. She's just another good-looking, copper-colored dog, adopted from a shelter. But inside there's a mountainful of love, courage, gratitude, and *joie de vivre*. It's inside her, it's inside all animals, and it's inside of us. We're glad it found expression in a dog named Penny.

Killing Them Softly

JEANIE ROBINSON-POWNALL

NO TIME IS EVER RIGHT FOR DEATH. At five o'clock on that cold and gloomy morning I could fully understand why winter symbolizes death. Lynda and I drove the eleven lonely miles between her dormitory and the animal shelter in almost complete isolation. The early hour and the lack of traffic combined with the quieting effect of a thick blanket of newly fallen snow to create an eerie stillness. The high banks of snow on either side of the northern New York road obstructed our peripheral vision, so the effect was the same as driving through an unending tunnel. We played the radio and sang along as loudly as we could, pretending that our pre-dawn journey was an ordinary, every day occurrence for two college co-eds, and not the mission of mercy and death it was.

As we neared the animal shelter, Lynda snapped off the radio. She'd been through this before and wanted to prepare me as best she could.

"The first one is over before you know it; it happens so fast that you're finished before your brain has had a chance to register it. It's in-between the first and second one that you have time to think," she added, "and that's when it's bad."

I nodded mutely, and the nervous, queasy, hungry-but-it-was-too-early-to-eat feeling in my stomach intensified.

Mentally I reviewed the sad statistics. Depending on your

source, some 10 to 20 million dogs and cats are euthanized every year in the United States because no one wants them. These are the more fortunate of the unwanted and abandoned; countless others starve to death, die of disease or under the wheels of a car, end up in the living hell of a research laboratory, or meet with a variety of other unpleasant and painful endings. Lynda and I were on our way to "help." As seniors studying for a degree in veterinary science technology, we possessed technical skills that were of use. We were coming to the animal shelter in the early morning darkness to put twenty-two dogs and cats to sleep. Then, before the civilized world that had abandoned these animals was even up and about, we would slip away.

Lynda was right. The first shaggy dog, someone's discarded pet, was dead in my arms before I could comprehend it. She struggled in fear, and urinated and moved her bowels as the life slipped from of her. Not even the dignity of a trip outside to relieve herself, I railed to myself. "What am I doing here?" I cried to Lynda. "I love animals and I want to work in the veterinary field to help them, not to kill the young and healthy ones!"

"It's not our fault!" Lynda's voice was fierce; she was battling her own pain while trying to be strong for me at the same time. "We're not really the ones doing it, Jean-Jean. It's those damned irresponsible people who don't honor or take seriously their commitment to their animals—that's whose killing them, not us. We give the injections, but the owners sign the death certificates when they forsake their responsibilities and leave their animals here."

As I reached for the second animal on the list, a little Dachshund with liquid eyes, I froze. I crouched on the floor, unable to move, one hand extended toward the worried animal. The shelter's one paid employee, the kennel cleaner, broke the spell.

"Don't be scared, he ain't gonna bite ya," he scoffed.

"I know he won't," I responded forcefully. "I'm not worried about being bitten. I just can't fathom why *someone* doesn't want this nice dog."

"There aren't enough 'someones,' Jean-Jean," Lynda responded softly.

I turned my attention back to the little Dachshund. I realized it would be easier for him—and us—if I focused on gaining the animal's trust first. That way there wouldn't be any struggle or fear, and he—and the others—could peacefully go to sleep in our arms.

I spoke to the little Dachshund. "Come to me, honey, come to me. No one's going to hurt you." Liar. With a whimper of hope, the dog came to me as I held out both arms to welcome him. I gathered him into my arms and he wiggled and cried with pleasure, and licked my cheek. He wanted so badly to love and be loved. Abandoned though he was, he was willing to trust again.

"Maybe…," I started to say to Lynda.

"No," she quietly but firmly cut me off. "You already have three dogs. You can't take in every stray that comes your way."

Lynda gently took the dog from me, placed him on the table facing me, and handed me the clippers. I kept talking to him as I shaved a patch of fur from the skin over his vein. His tail made a rhythmical "wap, wap, wap" on the table. He was anxious, but happy to have found a friend.

I carefully inserted the needle's tip into his vein. Suddenly the image of a smaller, younger me entered my mind. I long ago forgot the crime, but my mother's words have remained with me. *"The worst thing you can ever do is to betray someone who trusts you."*

Tears filled my eyes and streamed down my cheeks as I aspirated the syringe and pushed the plunger down. May God forgive us all: Those who abandon animals without remorse, and those who perform euthanasia against the dictates of our consciences.

The Starfish Story

A FRIEND OF MINE was walking along a Florida Beach the morning after Hurricane Cassandra had struck. As he walked along the water's edge, he saw that the storm's frenzied waves, howling winds and torrid rains had washed thousands of starfish up onto the beach. They lay stranded on the sand, in danger of dying from the sun's relentless rays beating down on them. Just then he noticed a lone figure at the other end of the beach, stooping and standing, stooping and standing, again and again. As he approached the figure he realized it was a woman, and that she was picking up starfish one by one, and throwing them back into the water.

When he was near enough to speak to the woman, he said to her, "Look at how many hundreds of starfish there are dying on the sand. How do you think that what you are doing can possibly make a difference?"

Once again she bent down, picked up another starfish, and as she tossed it into the ocean, she replied simply, "It makes a difference to this one."

Until he extends the circle of his compassion
to all living things,
man will not himself find peace.

ALBERT SCHWEITZER (1875-1965)

ABOUT THE
CONTRIBUTORS

Diane Allevato serves as Executive Director of the Marin Humane Society in Novato, California.

Diana M. Barrett is an Animal Control Officer with the Animal Control Section of the Oakland Police Department in Oakland, California.

Laura Bevan is director of the Southeast Regional Office of the Humane Society of the United States. The Florida Veterinary Medical Association named her "Citizen of the Year" for her work in the aftermath of Hurricane Andrew. She lives in Tallahassee, Florida.

Kelly Budner has worked as a veterinary assistant and is now a horse ranch manager in Evergreen, Colorado.

Joan V. Chadwick works as a humane educator for the British Columbia Society for the Prevention of Cruelty To Animals in Salmon Arm, south-central British Columbia.

Rosann Clay currently lives in North Richland Hills, Texas. She is a former member of the board of directors of the Murray/Calloway County Humane Society and volunteer at the Calloway County Animal Shelter in Murray, Kentucky.

KimberLee Curtis currently works as a director at WBIR-TV in

Knoxville, Tennessee. She has worked as an animal shelter adoption counselor, kennel worker, and animal control officer.

Cheryl L. Cutsforth has been a volunteer for two Wisconsin humane organizations. She has served as president, vice-president, recording secretary, and publications editor, and has helped with fundraising and foster care. She works as a librarian at the University of Wisconsin-Eau Claire.

Gary Dungan has worked in animal welfare for twenty years, serving in various capacities for the Denver Dumb Friends League, the Boulder County Humane Society, the Humane Society of Tucson, and the Valley Oaks SPCA, where he is now Executive Director.

Jan Elster is a management consultant who provides workshops and training for animal protection agencies, and businesses that benefit animals. She worked as a volunteer dog walker for the Marin Humane Society in Novato, California and was active in their animal assisted therapy program.

Ronnette Fish is General Manager of the Sioux Falls Humane Society. She has worked for the organization since 1984, serving prior to that as a volunteer and on the organization's board of directors.

Paul Glassner is the editor of *Our Animals,* the publication of the San Francisco Society for the Prevention of Cruelty To Animals in San Francisco, California.

Michelle LaRoux is a staff member at the Oshkosh Animal Shelter in Oshkosh, Wisconsin.

Dan S. Leavitt is a Humane Officer in Del Norte County, California and a recipient of the 1989 Golden Link Humane Officer of the Year Award. He resides in Crescent City, California.

Diane W. LeCrone has worked in a variety of volunteer and paid capacities for the Halifax Humane Society and the Flagler County Humane Society. She lives in Ormond Beach, Florida.

Therese C. MacKinnon is an Animal Care Technician at the privately run Robert Potter League for Animals, in Newport County, Rhode Island.

Joan Margalith is Director of Editorial and Public Affairs at radio station KCBS in San Francisco, California, and a volunteer for the San Francisco Society for the Prevention of Cruelty to Animals.

Tom Marksbury, at the time his piece was written, worked as a California State Humane Officer for the Marin Humane Society in Novato, California.

Pat Miller is Operations Director at the Marin Humane Society. She is a California State Humane Officer, a board member of the California Animal Control Director's Association, a co-founder of the Collective Humane Action and Information Network (C.H.A.I.N.), and she serves as editor of the *C.H.A.I.N. Letter.*

Julie Ann Mock serves as Treasurer of the Animal Shelter Assistance Program (ASAP), a unique non-profit support organization. ASAP provides funding and volunteers to benefit the cat population at the municipal animal shelter in Santa Barbara, California.

Laura Moretti is the Founder and Editor of *The Animals' Voice Magazine.* She lives in Chico, California.

Kathy Nash is a volunteer at the Marin Humane Society in Novato, California. She works in a variety of capacities, but specializes in reuniting lost pets with their owners.

Graham Phalen, a former Investigative Officer for the Arizona Humane Society, is currently studying law at the University of Arizona in Tucson.

Nancy P. Richards is the Administrator of the Southeast Missouri Humane Society in Cape Girardeau, Missouri. She holds degrees in criminal justice and sociology, and is currently taking courses in pre-veterinary medicine with hopes of studying to be a veterinarian.

Gina Richey is a humane officer for the Sherwood Department of Animal Control in Little Rock, Arkansas.

Mike Rowell is a writer for the San Francisco SPCA's *Our Animals.*

Jeanie Robinson-Pownall has worked as a volunteer cruelty investigator for the Allegheny County SPCA in Swain, New York, and as a veterinary technician. She lives in West Bradford, Pennsylvania.

Amy Shapiro, a former staff member at both the San Francisco SPCA and Peninsula Humane Society in California, now lives in Barboursville, Virginia, where she operates an animal sanctuary.

Karen Shea attends veterinary school at the University of Minnesota in St. Paul. She has worked at both the Cocheco Humane Society in New Hampshire and the Robert Potter League for Animals in Rhode Island.

Jennifer Sotelo is an Animal Care Technician at the Humane Society of Boulder Valley in Boulder, Colorado.

Anne Speakman lives in Montevallo, Alabama. She has worked in a variety of frontline and administrative capacities for humane organizations throughout Alabama.

Ward P. Sterling, a California State Humane Officer, worked for the Peninsula Humane Society in San Mateo, California. He is currently an officer with the California Highway Patrol in Ventura, California.

Diana B. Tidd has been a volunteer for the Humane Society of Southeast Missouri for seven years, participating in all aspects of the organization's activities, from newsletter editing and fundraising, to animal care and fostering.

Dawn Wallace is a Veterinary Technician at the Arizona Humane Society.

L. Dianne Washek is a nurse, and serves as Vice-President of Greyhound Friends, Inc. She lives in Ashland, Massachusetts.

Rebecca D. Winter is an Oregon writer. She volunteers at a municipal animal shelter, assisting in all aspects of shelter operations.

SOURCE NOTES

The following works have been previously published as noted:

"A Christmas Carol" and "Hello Dolly" by Diane Allevato first appeared in the Marin Humane Society's *Animal Tracks*.

"Andrew's Wake" by Laura Bevan originally appeared as "Struggle and Triumph in Andrew's Wake" in *HSUS News*.

"I Found Your Dog the Other Night" by Kelly Budner first appeared in *HSUS News* as "Happy Holidays."

"The Sentinel" and "Sage" by Ronnette Fish both originally appeared in the Sioux Falls Humane Society's *Tattle Tails*.

"The Real Cinderella" by Paul Glassner originally appeared in the San Francisco Society for the Prevention of Cruelty to Animals' (SF/SPCA) *Our Animals* as "From Pauper to Princess."

"Roundup at Rowdy Creek" by Dan S. Leavitt first appeared in the *C.H.A.I.N.* (Collective Humane Action and Information Network) *Letter*.

Joan Margalith's "Penny's Shine" was originally published as "The Caring Difference" in the SF/SPCA's *Our Animals*.

"Whisper" by Tom Marksbury first appeared in the *C.H.A.I.N. Letter*.

Pat Miller's "Kitten Season Again" appeared in the *C.H.A.I.N. Letter* and *Paws for Thought* (B.J. Ellis, *Paws for Thought: A Look at the Conflicts, Questions, and Challenges of Animal Euthanasia* [Columbia: Paw Print Press, 1993]). "The Night Before Christmas Shelter Style" and "Eulogy to Scotty Lightfoot" have both appeared in the *C.H.A.I.N. Letter*.

"Firestorm Diary" by Kathy Nash first appeared in the Marin Humane Society's *Animal Tracks*.

"How Kato Was Rescued From the Superstition Mountains" by Graham Phalen was first published as "Horse Flown to Safety After Week Long Effort in the Superstition Mountains" in *Arizona Humane Society* magazine.

"Faith and a Dog Named Max" by Mike Rowell was originally printed as "Max Comes Through" in the SF/SPCA's *Our Animals*.

"For Gray Cat" by Amy Shapiro first appeared in the Peninsula Humane Society's *Pawprint* as "Saying Good-by Every Day."

"Against All Odds" by Jennifer Sotelo has appeared as "Battling the Odds at the Humane Society" in *DeTails*, the publication of the Humane Society of Boulder Valley, and as "One to Stand for Many Who Fall: Coming to Terms With Euthanasia" in the *C.H.A.I.N. Letter*.

"A Day in the Life" by Ward P. Sterling has previously appeared in the *C.H.A.I.N. Letter* and HSUS' *Shelter Sense*.

"The Starfish Story" is based loosely on "The Star Thrower," an essay by Loren Eisely published in his book by the same name. For many years variations of this inspiring tale have circulated among humane professionals and been shared at animal welfare conferences. The editor is particularly indebted to Sanora Kay Grambort and Pat Miller for suggesting its inclusion.

RESOURCES

FROM THE SMALLEST LOCAL animal shelters to the largest
national humane organizations, there exist a wide variety of
programs and resources for those interested in learning more about
and supporting companion animal welfare. The following pages
offer only a partial list of some important organizations and
valuable publications.

NATIONAL ORGANIZATIONS

American Humane Association (AHA)
63 Inverness Drive East
Englewood, CO 80112
(303) 792-9900
Operates relief operations for animals during natural disasters, conducts trainings and conferences for animal welfare professionals, monitors treatment of animal actors on sets, and lobbies on behalf of animals in Washington, D.C.

The Delta Society
P.O. Box 1080
Renton, WA 98057
(206) 226-7357
Human/animal bond research and education organization.

Humane Society of the United States (HSUS)
2100 L Street NW
Washington, D.C. 20037
(202) 452-1100
Monitors all aspects of animal welfare issues, assists local shelters and humane organizations through its ten Regional Offices, conducts conferences for animal welfare professionals, aids in animal relief efforts during natural disasters, promotes humane education, and produces and sells a variety of materials on all aspects of animal welfare.

The Latham Foundation
Latham Plaza Building
Clement & Schiller Streets
Alameda, CA 94501
(510) 521-0920
Promotes humane education and values through a variety of means. Produces and distributes wide range of films and videotapes on human/animal relationships and animal welfare issues.

The National Association for the Advancement of Humane &
Environmental Education (NAAHEE)
67 Salem Rd.
East Haddam, CT 06423
(203) 434-8666
*Promotes humane education in schools by publishing and distributing teaching
materials, and provides resources for humane education personnel at
community animal shelters.*

LOCAL RESOURCES

Most communities have either (and in many cases both) a municipal animal control facility (operated by the city or county) and a
private non-profit Humane Society or SPCA. While these local
humane organizations are often commonly identified as "humane
societies" and "societies for the prevention of cruelty to animals,"
they are *independent and self-sustaining entities*—they have no
parent organization nor do they benefit from funding from any
national source (although in many communities such organizations *do* receive some government funding by providing animal
control services under contract for local municipalities). These
organizations may be found in the government section of the tele-
phone book or under "Animal Shelters" or "Humane Societies" in
the yellow pages of the phone book. Volunteer opportunities are
usually plentiful, and funds are always needed to improve services
and programs. **Supporting local humane organizations and
programs is the single most direct and important action anyone
can pursue to improve companion animal welfare in their community.**

There are many simple but effective personal steps everyone can
take to contribute to companion animal welfare. Those of us who

own pets or those of us who plan to add a pet to our family should make lifetime commitments to our animals. Studies reveal a disturbingly high percentage of family pets do not live out their full lives in their original home. Many are passed from home to home numerous times. All too often such animals eventually end up surrendered to a humane shelter.

Making sure we are responsible pet owners is an important part of promoting companion animal welfare. Spaying and neutering all pets, insuring they are always wearing clear identification, and, if it is required, a license, keeping animals vaccinated, making sure they do not roam, and obeying all local animal ordinances, especially leash laws, will benefit all the animals in our communities.

Most importantly, we can all contribute to improving the welfare of companion animals if we adopt our pets from community animal shelters, and encourage everyone we know to do the same.

PUBLICATIONS

The following newsletters, journals, and other regularly published resources are listed by organization.

The American Humane Association:

Shoptalk
- Newsletter for animal control professionals

Advocate
- Membership magazine

Contact:
The American Humane Association
63 Inverness Drive East
Englewood, CO 80112
(303) 792-9900

Collective Humane Action and Information Network (C.H.A.I.N.):

C.H.A.I.N. Letter
- Comprehensive journal of recent and ongoing neglect and cruelty cases and investigations, essays by humane professionals, and detailed news from the animal welfare field. Primarily intended for those working in the field, but it should be of interest to all those who care about animal welfare issues.

Contact:
Collective Humane Action and Information Network (C.H.A.I.N.)
% Cindy Machado
Marin Humane Society
171 Bel Marin Keys Blvd.
Novato, CA 94949

The Delta Society:

Interactions
- Membership magazine on human/animal bond issues

Anthrozoös
  ◆ Scholarly journal on human/animal relationships
Contact:
  The Delta Society
  P.O. Box 1080
  Renton, WA 98057
  (206) 226-7357

Humane Society of the United States:
Shelter Sense
  ◆ Publication for animal shelter personnel
HSUS News
  ◆ Membership and news magazine

Contact:
  Humane Society of the United States
  2100 L Street NW
  Washington, D.C. 20037
  (202) 452-1100

The Latham Foundation:
The Latham Letter
  ◆ Membership newsletter publishes studies, reports, essays, and
  book reviews on all aspects of humane education and animal
  welfare.

Contact:
  The Latham Foundation
  Latham Plaza Building
  Clement & Schiller Streets
  Alameda, CA 94501
  (510) 521-0920

BOOKS

The following is a sampling of some books on the relationship between companion animals and humans, and animal welfare issues. Some of these books have been around for a number of years—and a few are no longer in print—but they all offer fascinating insights into our attitudes toward and treatment of pets.

Beck, Alan, Sc.D. and Aaron Katcher, M.D., *Between Pets and People* (New York: Perigee Books, 1983).
  ◆ Out of print but available through libraries. Fascinating exploration of why we keep and care about pets

Carson, Gerald, *Men, Beasts and Gods: A History of Cruelty and Kindness to Animals* (New York: Charles Scribner's Sons, 1972).
  ◆ Out of print but available through libraries. One of the best historical accounts of human conduct towards animals and the development of the humane movement.

Fox, Dr. Michael A., *Inhumane Society: The American Way of Exploiting Animals* (New York: St. Martin's Press, 1990).
  ◆ A thorough and detailed examination of contemporary animal welfare issues.

Morris, Desmond, *The Animal Contract* (New York: Warner Books, 1990).
  ◆ A wide-ranging and informative work on all aspects animal welfare and rights issues.

Serpell, James, *In the Company of Animals* (New York: Basil Blackwell, 1986).
  ◆ A fascinating history of human relationships with and attitudes towards other species, with special attention towards pets.

Turner, E.S., *All Heaven in a Rage* (London: Michael Joseph, 1964).
  ◆ Recently re-issued by Centaur Press, this is a classic history of the early animal protection movement.

White, Betty and Thomas J. Watson, *Betty White's Pet Love* (New York: William Morrow and Company, 1983).
  * Informal look at the value of animal companionship.

Wynne-Tyson, Jon, ed., *The Extended Circle: A Commonplace Book of Animal Rights* (New York: Paragon House, 1989).
  * An anthology of quotes about compassion and human conduct towards other species by noted philosophers and activists throughout history.

Today a great many more books are being published on the relationship between humans and animals and on animal rights and welfare themes. Check your local bookstores and library and ask them to carry more titles on these topics.

ABOUT THE EDITOR

Elaine Sichel is an award-winning educator and consultant on animal welfare issues and the human-animal bond. She worked for many years at a humane society and has designed and taught workshops and college courses nationwide on the relationship between people and animals. She makes her home with her shelter-adopted dog Beau near the Sonoma Coast in Northern California.

ABOUT THE PHOTOGRAPHER

After a successful eighteen-year career as a photographer for two Michigan newspapers, Sumner W. Fowler turned his focus to the field of animal welfare. Fourteen years ago, after working for humane organizations in Ann Arbor and San Francisco, he joined the staff of The Marin Humane Society in Novato, California.

VOICE & VISION
Publishing

VOICE & VISION Publishing was founded in 1993.
Its mission is to foster greater awareness and
compassion by bringing to print and a wider
audience the words and images of those who
work on behalf of humane values.

❧

A portion of the proceeds from this book will be distributed
among the organizations whose stories are featured.

ORDERING INFORMATION

To order additional copies of
Circles of Compassion: A Collection of Humane Words and Work,
send a check or money order for $12 (plus $2.50 for shipping and
handling for the first book, 75¢ for each additional book) to:

VOICE & VISION Publishing
12005 Green Valley Rd.
Sebastopol, CA 95472

Please add 7.5% sales tax to orders shipped within California.

PLEASE ALLOW 3-4 WEEKS FOR DELIVERY

*If you represent a non-profit organization or business interested in
purchasing copies of this book for fundraising or resale purposes, please
write the publisher for detailed discount information.*